LOOK TO THE
MOUNTAINS
– My help comes from the Lord...

Stories of Kagando Hospital
and Rural Development Centre, Uganda

Told by Rob and Jen Morris

ISBN: 978-1-907636-99-8

Published by Verité CM Ltd for Rob and Jen Morris
Cover design, typesetting and production management
by Verité CM Ltd, Worthing, West Sussex UK
+44 (0) 1903 241975

Acknowledgements

Many people have helped to bring this book together, and we are so grateful to them all. It is difficult to single out individuals, but thanks are particularly due to Margaret Sentamu, Janet Muhindo, Jehoshaphat Bwalhuma, Ruth, Philip, Esther and Stephen for their advice, practical help, correcting historical detail, and proof reading.

Psalm 121 A Song of Ascents

1 I lift up my eyes to the mountains –
   where does my help come from?
2 My help comes from the Lord,
   the Maker of heaven and earth.
3 He will not let your foot slip –
   he who watches over you will not slumber;
4 indeed, he who watches over Israel
   will neither slumber nor sleep.
5 The Lord watches over you –
   the Lord is your shade at your right hand;
6 the sun will not harm you by day,
   nor the moon by night.
7 The Lord will keep you from all harm –
   he will watch over your life;
8 the Lord will watch over your coming and going
   both now and forevermore.

Esyonyimbo 121

1 Ngasamalira oko bitwa;
  Ko buwatikya bwage bwasyaluahi kwehi?
2 Obuwatikya bwage bukalua oko Mwami Mukulu,
  Oyo wahangika olubula n'ekihugo.
3 Sialeke ngatoga;
  Omuhanganiri wage sialiyato!
4 Omuhanganiri wa Israeli;
  Sialiyitsingirako kutse eriyato!
5 Omwami Mukulu asyakuteya;
  Omwami Mukulu ali oko luhande lwawe
  erikuhanganire.
6 Eryuba siryendikwagalya omo musibo,
  Kutse omukera omo kiro.
7 Omwami Mukulu asyakuhanganira omo bwiko bosi;
  Asyakuteya buholo.
8 Omwami Mukulu asyakuhanganira omugulu ukahika,
  n'omugulu ukahuluka,
  Eritsuka lino n'erihika kera na kera.

About the Authors

Rob and Jen Morris are the third generation in their respective families to have served as missionaries in the past 100 years in Africa. Their lives have been enriched by their experiences and the close relationships they have made through their time in Uganda.

For the last 27 years they have lived and worked in Handcross, Sussex, UK. Jen working as a Practice Nurse, and Rob as a General Medical Practitioner. They are involved in their local Parish Church of St Mary's, Slaugham, where Rob serves as a Lay Reader.

Their four children with their spouses have all been full time Christian workers in places as far flung as Wales, Darfur (Sudan), Nepal and New Zealand. They have eleven grandchildren.

They continue to be closely linked to the work at Kagando, and are trustees of the charity, Friends of Kagando.

Contents

Foreword

Jesus said to his followers, "I have come that you may have life in all its fullness" (John 10:10). As a young girl growing up in Uganda poverty was never a theory, something you read about in textbooks or reports. I grew up alongside people who lived on less than 50p ($1) a day and this was their daily reality. There are still many families who have to manage on one meal a day; who have to walk for miles to get clean water, and several miles to find not a doctor but a nurse auxiliary, with a handful of aspirins, if they are lucky, and who cannot afford to buy malaria tablets. It is for such families as these that missionaries and expatriates over the past decades have given up the comforts of their home countries to go and serve in countries like Uganda in order that others might simply live. As someone who benefitted hugely from the work of missionaries and expatriates who responded to the call, I am always very impressed by the sacrifice and commitment of these men and women and their families.

In this book marking the 50th Anniversary of the Kagando Project, both Jen and Rob Morris, both children of missionaries, speak movingly of God's faithfulness to the Kagando project and the way God used people and circumstances to work out His good plans. It is quite obvious that it has not been all plain sailing but the stories told here are of men and women who 'clung' onto God through thick and thin. I hope that as you read these stories you will feel inspired and encouraged to do your bit in responding to what God is calling you to do and to become. We give thanks for the past, offer to God the present and the future knowing that we are surrounded by a great cloud of witnesses who have gone on before us to bear the good news of our Lord Jesus Christ, in all its fullness.

Margaret Sentamu, MA in Adult Education with Theology
Bishopthorpe, York
Patron of Friends of Kagando Charity
Principal Consultant and Head of Diversity at
Odgers & Berndtson
Lay adjudicator for the Solicitors Regulatory Authority
Independent member of the Disciplinary Competency
Scheme of CIPFA
Non-Executive Director of Traidcraft Plc

*   *   *

Ten dusty asbestos huts and a mud brick building were all that confronted Keith Waddell when he arrived at Kagando Hospital in 1964. There, in the shadow of the Blue Mountains, this young missionary doctor set out on a life of frugal living and dedicated Christian service: tending the sick, restoring sight, and affording education for innumerable young African people.

This book tells the story of God's blessing as Keith and the faithful men and women following him transformed Kagando's sparse facilities into a thriving hospital – and much, much more.

Professor Richard Vincent, BSc MD FRCP FESC AKC
Chief Executive Officer, PRIME
Founding Director of the Trafford Centre for Graduate
Medical Education and Research at Sussex University
Had a key role in designing and running the Brighton and
Sussex Medical School.

"Look to the Mountains" is a wonderful collection of real life stories of the witness of men and women who chose to seek to glorify God by living out in difficult conditions in a remote area of Uganda! Dr Rob and Jen Morris, with their four children, were dear family friends; my two sisters were co-workers with this unorthodox yet lovely couple who lived out their loyalty, commitment and love for God.

As you read this book, you will be fascinated by the couple's faith through their daily risk taking experiences, for themselves and for their children. Don't miss out on when they put on many hats attempting to manage the crisis of a disorientated society.

Kagando hospital, and then KARUDEC, has been used by God to meet the physical, emotional, mental and spiritual needs of many. Rob and many of his colleagues who came earlier and later to Kagando worked tirelessly to ensure God was the centre of all activities. Prayer was central within the hospital including when starting a car! The hospital trained nurses, drivers and other workers on the job, developing skills in many people; they built teams for spiritual outreach, choirs and managers of poultry, agriculture, forestry, building on the rich God given gifts found in the Bakonzo community. It is no surprise that the name Kagando Hospital grew from just a hospital to Kagando Rural Development Centre (KARUDEC).

Uganda suffered terribly during years of misrule and civil war; under God's hand, Kagando survived and served many and remains today a witness to God's faithfulness in a wicked world.

This thoughtful and extremely practical book takes you through the miracles God does, using his mortal children on earth. It may change your attitude about your view of how God works in the world today. It may influence you to think twice on how best you can use your God given talent, which you have ignored for ages, or cause you to think of someone who needs to be approached. If it prompts you to pray, please do, because it is a faith taking experience that enables you test God for whom He is.

Rev Canon Janet Muhindo, Assistant Provincial Education Co-ordinator, and in charge of Church of Uganda's children's programmes until she retired in 2013.

*   *   *

Kagando, 18 October 2014

As we drove off from the airfield at Kasese in July 1980, I was surprised at how many people our driver knew. At just 21 years old, this was my first time in Africa, let alone Uganda. We kept on waving to people as we drove past them at the side of the road. 'Hello' we would say, smiling. But after a while, we got too tired of this and just waved. Only slowly did it dawn on me that these were not people our hosts knew at all. It's just that everyone greets each other in these friendly Rwenzori foothills. This was just the first of many culture shocks I experienced at Kagando. Green bananas, cassava, marching ants, and neatly cut *Guardian Weekly* newspaper sheets for toilet paper, were others.

The Bible Society was founded in 1804. The first society of its kind to exist, it was founded by the same people who abolished slavery in the British Empire. As the leader of this society today, I can trace my own interest in offering the Bible to the world to my time spent at Kagando. Soon after the ending of the Amin regime, when Tanzanian troops were occupying the country, I was a member of the first Tear Fund student summer team. Those two months at Kagando Hospital were a life-changing experience for me, and I owe so much to the people who served at the hospital and the projects associated with it. Part of my work was to conduct a survey of the health conditions of the people living in the region south of Kasese near Lake George. I discovered that one in four children died before they were eleven.

One day we walked miles up into one of the most remote places I have ever been. Had a European ever walked these paths before? At the very top of one of the highest hills, we visited the simple home of an elderly man with failing sight. He claimed to be over 100 years old and had seen Henry Morton Stanley (an early explorer to Uganda in 1880s) ride into Fort Portal on a camel. Remarkably, the maths do work out.

When I arrived with two colleagues he warmly welcomed us and told me his story. He was glad to say how he had become a Christian as a young man, but that he didn't have a Bible of his own any more. As the most valuable item he owned, apparently his son had stolen it from him and taken it across the border to the DRC (Democratic Republic of Congo) to sell. That was many years before. The one thing this frail man wanted in life was to have a Bible of his own. The next day we took a Good News Bible to him and he was thrilled. I can see his bright and burning eyes still. This was one of the greatest privileges of my life and set me on a path that has brought me to Bible Society today. Sadly, many homes in Uganda are still without the Scriptures. It's a culture shock that none of us should have to experience today. And it remains one of the greatest challenges of our time.

James Catford is Group Chief Executive of the British and Foreign Bible Society, Vice-chair of Amity Printing Company (the largest manufacturer of the Bible in the world), chair of Renovaré Britain & Ireland, ministry team member of Renovaré US, and a senior fellow of the Dallas Willard Centre at Westmont College, Southern California.

Introduction

"Nothing was achieved without
human commitment.
Nothing was achieved without
divine involvement" [1]

In 1979 there was little more than the hospital compound, some lodgings that served visiting patients, one or two tiny shops, and a few scattered homesteads that made up the village of Kagando. It was to this that we, Rob & Jen, came to serve under the "umbrellas" of both TEAR Fund and Africa Inland Mission. We shared a background of growing up as the children of missionaries in East Africa. Born in Akobo, Sudan, Jen spent a significant part of her childhood in Kabale, South West Uganda. Born in Eldoret, Kenya, Rob's parents were later serving as missionaries in Tanzania when at the age of seven he started his first school, also in Kabale. But it was not until two years later that we met as fellow pupils at St Andrews' School, Turi, in Kenya. In the relatively small world of Christian missionary work in East Africa, and Evangelical Christian Ministry in the UK, it is not altogether surprising that our parents and grandparents were good friends. Later on, as Christian students studying Medicine and Nursing in London, it was hardly surprising that we would meet again sooner or later, and so it happened in 1969.

---

1   Goldingay 1&2 Chronicles; writing about the building of
    Solomon's temple.

Our friendship became a courtship, and we started to talk about marriage; right from the beginning we shared a conviction that God had called us, and was equipping us to serve together in a mission environment. As we finished undergraduate and then postgraduate training nine years later, now married and with three little children, we experienced God's clear call again. We were challenged and encouraged by our church at that time, All Saints' Lindfield, UK, to look beyond the local needs. And so we applied in 1978 to serve with TEAR Fund in their Overseas Personnel programme to work wherever they felt that God was sending us. That turned out to be a secondment to Africa Inland Mission, to work at Kagando Hospital, near Kasese, in Western Uganda.

In January 2015 Kagando Hospital will be 50 years old. Built as a leprosy settlement, it was taken over in January 1965 by Africa Inland Mission at the invitation of the Uganda Government of the time. Since then Kagando has served the communities of this part of Western Uganda in the shadows of the Rwenzori Mountain range, as a hospital providing medical care for some of the world's most poor and neglected people. Over the years the hospital has grown, extended its range of service through education, agriculture, community health outreach and the provision of gravity fed clean water. It is completely run by Ugandan leaders under the umbrella of the Church of Uganda, with Uganda Government and overseas support.

This book is part of the story of God's remarkable intervention and provision in this remote hospital in a very needy part of Uganda. The stories are about a just and loving God who takes the initiative – Kagando is part of His story – but who in His grace uses frail and faulty human beings to fulfil His purpose and plan. It is one of the great mysteries – that God takes rebellious people whom He loves and forgives. Then He recruits them to share in a plan for restoration of His creation, which will end in Christ's return. Then there will be no more injustice, pain or death. God's uses human beings and their contributions as part of this restoration plan.

Writing this book together, we know that we are very privileged with the backgrounds, education, love and support that we have enjoyed all our lives, although we have also known pain. We have shared both personally and through our work in situations that are profoundly unjust, bereavements that tear the hearts out of good people, and failed relationships that scar and distort what should otherwise be beautiful and productive. There are many things that we don't understand, but we see in the story of Kagando so much that illustrates God's way of dealing with mankind. In the words of a card that was given to Rob after his father was killed in a car accident: "Father, I don't understand, but I trust you".

We hope that you will enjoy some of the stories that have made Kagando what it is today.

*   *   *

Rita Miller is a trustee of Friends of Kagando, a UK charity set up to support the work of Kagando, and this is part of her story:

"Over the years I have watched numerous heart breaking scenes on TV where healthcare in developing countries is stretched and aid workers battle with limited resources to overcome horrific epidemics or natural disasters. I would sit there wondering how I could be of help and then end up switching it off in frustration and sadness. Then in the autumn of 2008 I realised that I do have the ability and skills to be of some help, so I should do something about it! I am a practice nurse and as Chair of the Yorkshire Practice Nurses I was able to get the support and encouragement of the committee, including my friend, Chris, to start up Yorkshire Practice Nurse Aid.

The challenge now was to find a charity that we could support! We began to look for contacts in the third world which our group could help.

In February 2009 I shared our vision of getting involved in overseas work with a friend who told me about a plastic surgeon he knew who had worked in a hospital called Kagando in Uganda. After some research into the hospital and charity, Friends of Kagando, I decided that this was the place we should choose. I called Chris the following day but before I could tell her about my findings she said she had found that her church was supporting a physiotherapist in Africa who was a missionary and that she thought that this was the right place for us to be involved. It was a place called Kagando! Of all the hospitals in the world where we might have gone, we were both led to this same place on the same weekend by completely different contacts. We felt that someone somewhere was pointing us in that direction. We could not ignore this place...

...and the rest is history"

As we write this, Rita is working at Kagando, serving as a nurse in the hospital, community and nurses' training school (struggling with an outbreak of Marburg Disease, a viral illness similar to and only slightly less lethal than

Ebola Disease). Her story is not unique in its illustration of God's initiatives involving women and men, as they seek to co-operate with our great Protagonist[2] God in reaching out to a needy world. There are other stories like this in the history of Kagando, some of which are told here.

---

2 A protagonist (from Ancient Greek πρωταγωνιστής (protagonistes), meaning "one who plays the first part, chief actor")

CHAPTER ONE

Background to Kagando

'In all things God works for good...'[1]

In the 1950s there was little in the way of health care in rural parts of Uganda. Nyabirongo was and is a small village at the heart of the Bakonzo people, a neglected and deprived minority tribe, almost on the equator as it crosses the great continent of Africa. It is situated in the southern foothills of the Rwenzori Mountains which stretch 140 kilometres North from the equator, straddling the border between Uganda and Congo. A Government dispensary in Nyabirongo offered basic health care for the people who lived in the area. Leprosy was a big health and social problem, and the only way to manage patients who were infected with the disease was to isolate them from the rest of the community. Kagando, which was a collection of a dozen asbestos huts about 5 kilometres from Nyabiriongo, was an ideal place to house leprosy patients in isolation, as there was no one living in the area.

Hon Ezron Mbethe Bwambale, the deputy minister of culture in Uganda, a Mukonzo (member of the Bakonzo tribe), lived locally and he tried to help some of these leprosy patients, by transporting them across the border to Oicha in Eastern Congo, where an American missionary doctor named Carl Becker was working with Africa Inland

---

1   Romans 8:28

Mission. Two of these patients, Kibingo Manasse and Joseph Kabuthirwaki, both now in their 80s, still live in the area around Kagando, and remember being taken to the mission station at Oicha to be treated by the famous Dr Becker.

In the 1950's and '60's new effective treatments became available which meant that people with leprosy no longer had to be kept apart from the rest of the population. They were now treated in their communities, and so those asbestos huts and the other simple buildings at Kagando became redundant as the patients with leprosy moved back to their families in the mountains and valleys around.

By 1964 the political situation in eastern Congo was becoming increasingly unsettled. Known as the Simba ('lion') Rebellion, the movement appeared to be communist in its origin, backing and character. Christians, and especially missionaries, were particularly targeted, and it finally became too dangerous for the missionaries to continue to work in that area. Many missionaries were forced to leave the country, some were injured, others attacked, raped or killed.[2] In September 1964, Dr Carl and Mrs Marie Becker, with their missionary colleagues, had to escape for their lives across the border into Uganda, spending the first night after their escape in a hotel in Kasese.

The following day they travelled on to Kampala and received a warm welcome from the senior AIM missionaries, Harold and Jane Amstutz. Over the next few weeks they consulted with other missionary personnel and prayed for God's guidance for the future.

2   *Give me this Mountain* by Helen Roseveare

Some weeks later they heard that their hospital at Oicha had been ransacked and that all the 110 members of hospital staff had been evacuated out of Congo to a camp at Bundibugyo, inside Uganda. Two of the staff, medical assistants, Isaiah Kataliko and Yonama, travelled to Kampala to ask Dr Becker to help them find work temporarily. He insisted that it would be better if the two Africans meet with the Ugandan authorities and not an American missionary. He thought they should go to areas close to their homeland – Yonama to the North and Kataliko to the West.

Following this suggestion, Kataliko found the Member of Parliament for Toro South, the Honourable Ezron Bwambale, deputy minister for culture, who happened to be staying in Kampala at the time. Hon Bwambale had been part of a delegation invited to London in 1961 to write a constitution for Uganda prior to independence. Hon Bwambale and Kataliko held discussions about the possibility of finding a suitable place to use their medical skills. Hon Bwambale immediately thought of the great needs for improved health care in his home area of Busongora County near the Congo border.

The Beckers planned to travel over to the West of the country to visit their staff in the refugee camp. However, this part of Western Uganda was itself struggling with tribal unrest on the slopes of the Rwenzori Mountains. The Bakonzo were resentful of the neglect they continued to suffer under the newly formed Ugandan government, and had declared themselves an independent 'Rwenzururu United Kingdom'. As a result of this political instability, expatriates needed police permits to enter the area.

While the paperwork was being prepared for the Beckers, they were invited to dinner by Ezron Bwambale. During the meal he proposed that Dr Becker and his staff should expand the medical work being done in the Government health centre at Nyabiriongo. This unit had been excluded from the government health programme due to the tribal unrest in the area. The following day they met with the Minister of Health, who was well informed and friendly, and he encouraged them to consider the MPs suggestion.

Once the travel permits were ready, Hon Bwambale was eager to go with them and show them the place he had in mind. The last few kilometres of road leading to the Kagando site was narrow, and Kagando itself turned out to be a deserted leprosy settlement comprised of about 10 asbestos huts and 2 mud brick buildings. Dr Becker's immediate reaction was rather negative and he later wrote that "the place had been vandalised and was anything but attractive".

Seeing their disappointment, Ezron Bwambale took them five kilometres back to where, just off the road and hidden by tall grass, they found a small rural maternity centre and dispensary at Nyabirongo. It was being manned by one medical assistant and several midwives. He informed the Beckers that both sites were available for the missionaries to use for the development of health care if they would be prepared to take them on.

Back in Kampala Dr and Mrs Becker shared the ideas with the AIM leadership team. Both central Government and the Mukama (King) of Toro were in favour of starting a new hospital in the area and so permission was granted. Hon Bwambale succeeded in having the entire Oicha staff transferred from Bundibugyo to Nyabirongo, a distance of 160 kilometres. He was also instrumental in helping to clear Dr Beckers medical credentials with the Ugandan authorities.

Local chiefs and Church leaders became involved too and gave invaluable help in welcoming and resettling the medical team. Kataliko remembers the kind people there who generously brought food and other necessities to their new neighbours.

And so finally in January 1965, with a kerosene stove and refridgerator, two beds, a table, four chairs, a lantern, wash basins and some borrowed instruments, Carl and Marie Becker were ready to start work. Gradually more equipment came from overseas and the service to patients improved.

Both the Kagando and Nyabirongo sites were slowly repaired and cleaned up. Most of the medical work initially took place at Nyabirongo, while renovations and building work began at Kagando, again helped by Hon Bwambale who kindly donated a tractor and trailer.

The part that Honourable Ezron Bwambale played in the start of Kagando Hospital should not be under estimated. His vision, enthusiasm and persistence persuaded the Uganda Government, the Mukama, the missionaries and the local leaders to work together for the good of the vulnerable, poor and needy people living in the area.

Six months later, Dr Keith Waddell, a new recruit with Africa Inland Mission, who had been assigned to go to join Dr Becker in Congo, was now invited to come to Nyabirongo and Kagando. Keith well remembers his first trip to the area. Driving in a Hillman Husky car, he came to the Eastern edge of the rift valley after dark. Looking westwards across the plains he saw the full moon shining spectacularly clearly on the snow covered mountains in the distance. The mountain range he saw that night, the majestic Rwenzori mountains ("Mountains of the moon"), rising to their spectacular 5,000 metre snow covered peaks, rarely lose their cloud cover, so it was of particular significance that Keith saw them that night in all their splendour under the full moon. Little did he realise that he would have a link to this area for the next 50 years and more.

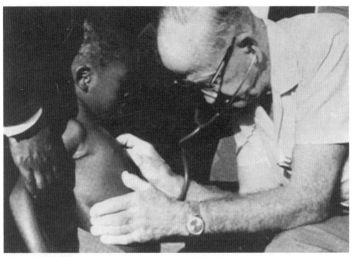

Dr Carl Becker examines a young child.

There continued to be political unrest in the area, and several Americans were expelled because of their nationality. One day Dr Becker received a message that he also would have to leave, but there was an outcry from the local people. The Bishop of Toro, Erica Sabiti, a Godly man (who was later to become the Archbishop of Uganda) went himself to see the then Archbishop Brown about the matter. He in turn went to see President Obote, and the eviction notice died a quiet death.

However, Dr Becker's heart was really fixed on Congo, and as soon as it seemed safe enough to return he said to Keith, 'This is a choice place, but we need to go, so you stay and look after (Kagando) for us'.

He later wrote about his months at Kagando in his autobiography, 'God's faithfulness' – "Our time there was eventful and fruitful. To us it was just another of those instances of God's preparing the way before us. Once again in the midst of turmoil, the Lord's great work of reconciliation spread out from this new centre". Before they left, the hospital evangelist recorded the names of over 500 people who had become Christians. Dr Becker is pictured opposite examining a child. Dr Keith Waddell, below, on his ward round.

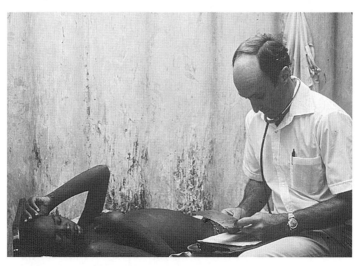

Most of the staff returned to Congo with Dr Becker towards the end of 1965, but a few stayed on and served Kagando for many more years. These included William Onali, a medical assistant from West Nile, Catherine a nurse from Congo, and Shadrack, the evangelist.

Patients began to come to the dispensary in increasing numbers for the good medical care they were given. A bus service between the border town of Bwera and Kasese was routed through Nyabirongo, bringing patients from further afield.

After working between the two sites for three years, it was decided to move the greater part of the medical work to Kagando. Each hut on the compound was a long, low asbestos building with a door at one end and a window at the other. The only source of light was from kerosene lanterns and limited lighting from the generator, which ran for 3 hours each evening. Eight of these huts were used as wards and the remaining smaller ones were for the patients' relatives who cooked their food on open fires. There was one whitewashed mud brick building with a large open veranda, which became the "intensive care ward" and maternity unit.

Jerry Rineer, an AIM missionary from the USA, came with his wife, Annie and their family to build an operating theatre and doctor's office at the Kagando site. He also put up a few staff houses, including an open plan one for their family and a small basic one roomed house for Keith, where he lived for many years. Its simplicity was more than made up for by the wonderful view of the mountains.

It was at this stage that the Nyabirongo site was transferred back into Government hands, but Kagando was given to the mission project, although it was not recognised as a hospital until 1967. The hospital and 100 acres of land were valued at 52,550 Uganda shillings, though disputes about the ownership of it continued for a further twenty years.

Keith took on the task of training nurse aids, following a programme that Carl Becker had started up very successfully in the Congo. Potential students who had completed seven years of primary education were interviewed and those who were accepted began a course of basic nurse training for two years. Some then progressed to train as 'writers' who were responsible for seeing the up to 500 patients who came to the outpatient clinic each day; they made diagnoses and gave appropriate treatments, then did the 'writing' up of the notes, referring on the more difficult cases. The brightest students could apply for further training to become medical assistants in government training schools, such as that in Fort Portal. Medical Assistants essentially carried out the work which a junior hospital doctor might do in developed countries.

Another feature of the early days were the monthly child immunisation clinics where, on a single day, up to 2000 children were registered, weighed and immunised at the hospital while the parents were given health advice, and a bar of soap for those who completed the course. Until the immunisation programme became really established in the wider community, a whole ward in Kagando Hospital would be almost constantly filled with children suffering from measles and its complications. Cases of polio, leprosy, meningitis, tetanus and malaria, and grotesque malnutrition, were also seen regularly. Profound anaemia in children due to a combination of Malaria, Hookworm and malnutrition was commonplace. Children often became malnourished at the age of two when their mother became pregnant with the next child, and stopped breastfeeding

There were also monthly antenatal clinics when around 500 expectant ladies, dressed in their best clothes, queued all day in the hot sun, in a line stretching as far as the eye could see for their antenatal checks. They did not seem to mind the wait and it became quite a social occasion for these women.

Another practice that was adopted from the AIM missionaries was the idea of a health insurance scheme. The plan was that each patient paid a few shillings to join the scheme and then they would receive free treatment for a whole year. The sums did not add up, however, and the hospital was soon struggling financially. The insurance scheme could not be sustained, and had to be replaced by a fee for service arrangement. Care was taken to try to ensure that, whether someone could afford to pay or not, all would be treated on the basis of need, not according to their means.

Kagando became a centre of excellent medical care for the poorest of the poor, delivered with appropriate use of simple technology and available resources. Keith's many skills as a physician, paediatrician, surgeon and ophthalmologist were greatly sought after, and patients came from near and far to receive treatment.

In 1967, Keith came down with hepatitis and went to South Africa for some months to recuperate. Visiting doctors came to fill in on this occasion, as at other times when he went on leave. These doctors included Hugh Maclure, Paget Stanfield and John Sandford Smith, each brilliant in his own specialty, and Keith developed additional skills from each. Most of the time, however, it was lonely work for Keith, as he worked on his own. He was ably supported by a succession of missionary nurses who worked alongside the doctors, teaching the nurse aids, and setting high standards of care and discipline.

At one time, patients stopped coming to the hospital because of the fear of the Rwenzururu soldiers in the mountains. Keith walked up to Buzira, in the mountains above Kagando, to meet with the Rwenzeruru leadership. He threatened to leave the hospital unless the intimidation of the local people stopped. Gradually things settled back down, but it was the first of several occasions when those at Kagando were involved in discussions about the need for peace and co-operation in the area. Arguably, Kagando played a vital role in preserving peace in the district.

A young medical student from the UK, named Richard Vincent, did his medical elective at Kagando in 1969. He went on to be an eminent cardiologist and professor of medicine in the UK, and later helped to found Brighton Medical School. He continues to be a faithful friend and supporter of Kagando to the present time.

In 1973, Keith became the official government leprosy adviser for the area, visiting clinics in a government leprosy control scheme, which became very successful in controlling the spread of the disease. It was at a time of great change in the treatment of leprosy and the new drug, dapsone, was used even before it became WHO policy. Keith's brilliance as a physician, his attention to detail, and meticulous record keeping all contributed to the effective control of this potentially devastating disease. Before the Leprosy control programme really started to work, Kagando had been among the world's worst places for the disease in terms of both new cases being diagnosed, and the prevalence of the disease in the community.

As the political tensions rose in Uganda under the leadership of President Idi Amin, at a time when one could be executed for carrying a jerry can of petrol, the staff helped the expatriates plan an emergency escape route over the mountains into Congo. 1977 was a particularly stressful year when the Archbishop of Uganda, Janani Luwum, was murdered. The following year all the British residents felt very vulnerable when the Queen celebrated her silver jubilee, and they expected they might have to leave at any time.

Towards the end of 1978 all the work at Kagando was under severe threat, and President Idi Amin's rule, with its uncertainties, dangers and extreme shortages, was taking its toll. The three missionaries serving at Kagando at that time were under great strain, utterly exhausted physically and emotionally.

When the Tanzanian army invaded Uganda from the South in early 1979, Keith and his colleagues accepted advice, and temporarily left the country.

CHAPTER TWO

Uganda – 'Pearl of Africa'[1]

"Can a nation be changed?
Can a nation be saved?
…Let this nation be saved…"[2]

There were tales in ancient Greece that 'the River Nile was fed by snow' and in AD 150, Ptolemy spoke of 'lunae montes' –'mountains of the moon' in central Africa which were covered with snow. However, it was not until 1862 that Speke, the first European explorer, arrived in the area, in his quest to find the source of the Nile. He referred to the mountain range as 'Rwenzori' meaning rainmaker in the local language. Some of the earliest explorers never saw the high mountains because of the continuous cloud cover over them. Water flows down from the mountains into Lake George, along the Kazinga Channel to Lake Edward which drains north into the Semliki River, through the Eastern Congo into Lake Albert, and from there, finally into the Nile.

Missionaries began to arrive in 1877 at the invitation of Mutesa, the Kabaka or King of Buganda – the largest and most influential tribal area in the country – after he met the explorer, Stanley. The Christian gospel was warmly received and quickly spread. However, his son,

---

1   Winston Churchill coined this title for Uganda

2   *Can a nation be changed?* Matt Redman, Worship Together.

Mwanga II who succeeded him, refused to believe in God, and turned on anyone with faith, whether Anglican, Catholic or Muslim. He ordered the murder of Bishop Hannington from the UK, and followed that up by killing anyone who showed more loyalty to God than they did to the King. Many of the young pages who served in his court accepted this new faith in Jesus Christ, and were secretly baptised. They then had to make a brave decision to break away from some of their old traditions. When they courageously refused the King's sexual advances, he was furious, and many were beheaded or burned alive. Rather than deter the growth of Christianity, the martyrdom of early believers seems to have sparked its growth. Martyr's Day, June 3rd, the day on which most of the martyrs were killed, is still celebrated each year in Uganda.

Germany, France and England were all keen to influence the future of Uganda, but in the end Uganda invited the British to oversee development in the country, and it became a British protectorate in 1894. The British were apparently largely motivated by a desire to protect the source of the Nile. Until this time the Kabaka was the absolute ruler of Buganda, from which Uganda derived its name.

In 1962, Uganda gained independence from Britain, and Milton Obote became the country's first Prime Minister. Under his leadership, there was a power struggle between him and the King of Buganda, who was eventually forced to escape from the country. Milton Obote then assumed the role of President, the constitution was changed, and Uganda became a republic. He proceeded to abolish all the kingdoms throughout the country, though he was unable to quash the Rwenzururu, as the rebel movement of the Bakonzo people became known. Obote remained in control of Uganda until 1971, when he was ousted by his own army commander, Idi Amin, who had served with the British army in the Kings African Rifles. While most of the country celebrated with the new leader, the euphoria did not last long, as it quickly became clear that anyone who was perceived as a threat to Idi Amin was quickly disposed of.

President Idi Amin's eight year rule started to come to an end early in 1979. All of Uganda's Asian community had been expelled in 1972, the economy was totally ruined, and at least 100,000 people had been murdered. He followed the example of the previous Ugandan leader, the Kabaka Mwanga, by not allowing any religions to exist in Uganda, except for Anglicans, Catholics and Muslims. He also murdered the Anglican Archishop, Janani Luwum, who refused to support Amin's brutality. The 'liberating' Tanzanian army helped rid Kampala of Amin in April 1979. But traumatised by President Amin's rule, then devastated by the invasion of the Tanzanian army from the south, Uganda remained troubled by war for a further six years. The country was led first by President Lule, then President Binaisa, followed briefly by a triumvirate that quickly broke up and left President Obote managing to return, and once again lead a now divided nation in 1981

The whole country, but Kampala in particular, remained very unstable and lawless for some years to come, with frequent outbursts of gunfire day and night. Stories of theft and violence were commonplace, and the shops were empty, or almost empty – in one shop we entered in 1980, the only thing for sale was a left shoe. There were few vehicles on the streets that did not belong to the army, and most of the population kept a low profile or else were still hiding in the bush. Compared to the estimated 100,000 murders committed by Idi Amin, some have estimated that Milton Obote went several steps further, killing around 500,000 of his countrymen during this period, largely on tribal grounds.

Most expatriates had left the country, with the exception of a few scattered communities, often missionary doctors and nurses manning church hospitals like Kagando.

CHAPTER THREE

Our arrival at Kagando in 1979

'My grace is all you need, for my power is strongest when you are weak' [1]

Privileged to have had parents and grandparents who had been missionaries, we were born and raised in rural parts of Africa. Rob's grandparents joined Africa Inland Mission (AIM), arriving at Mombasa in 1913 before embarking on the long 1,800 Kilometre journey on foot and horseback to Uganda, and then on to Eastern Congo. It was there that Rob's father, Philip, and his brothers, were born. Philip and his brother George were taken to school in Kenya each term by their father. Means of transport had developed, and they travelled on a motorbike and sidecar, sometimes stopping to shoot an elephant in order to sell the tusks, and so be able to pay for fuel and school fees. Trained as a doctor and later as an eye surgeon in the UK, Philip had had to overcome years of ill health in hospital due to a lung abscess in his teenage years. His remarkable recovery to achieve entry to medical school, and play rugby, tennis and hockey for King's Hospital, was a tribute to his determination and character.

Following his marriage to Mollie Salmon in 1947, they too went out to serve with AIM to Kenya in 1948 where Rob, their first child, was born. Some months later, when the family were on holiday and retracing Philip's childhood steps in Congo, baby Rob had a high fever and was taken to see the famous Dr Carl Becker for treatment in Oicha!

---

1 2 Corinthians 12.9

Jen's grandparents, Algie & Zoe Stanley Smith joined Church Missionary Society in 1920. They also travelled to Western Uganda where they were joint founder members of the Rwanda Mission and they remained as missionaries in Uganda until they were in their late 80s. Their eldest daughter, Nora, grew up planning to follow her parents into missionary work in Africa. Her fiancé, Dick Lyth, spent the war years in Southern Sudan. Initially serving as a missionary with CMS, Dick volunteered to serve with the Sudan Defence Force when the Second World War broke out. With his 120 Sudanese soldiers he successfully kept the Italians, based in Ethiopia, with their 120,000 troops, from invading Sudan, and taking control of the Nile.[2] After eventually marrying Nora, he continued to serve in Sudan as District Commissioner until the country gained independence in 1954. He then became ordained into the Anglican Church, and they went out as missionaries once again, this time to Uganda with Rwanda Mission. In 1967 Dick was consecrated as the first Bishop of Kigezi Diocese.

Idi Amin respected Bishop Dick Lyth as a fellow soldier, and they met on several occasions, usually when Dick was pleading for the life of one of his pastors. Amin said he always felt safe when Dick was standing behind him, as he was the only person he could trust not to put a bullet through him.

Towards the end of 1978 we, Jen and Rob, were in the midst of our preparations to leave for Uganda. Our family at that time consisted of ourselves, and our three children, Ruth, Philip and Esther (Stephen at that stage was a sixteen week unborn baby in his mother's womb!).

---

2 *The Red Pelican* Jon Arensen

Just a month before we were due to leave the UK, we received two very long, detailed letters from Lois Clark, one of the nurses at Kagando, describing the situation there in Uganda at that time. She wanted us to know what it was like before we arrived, and so she was very blunt about the difficulties, dangers and shortages. She wrote saying that there was no fuel or food or supplies of any kind in shops and petrol stations. Receiving this letter, we wondered again whether we should be going to Kagando, and if it was right to be exposing our three young children to such risk. Reading the verses set for that day in Daily Light we read 'my grace is all you need, for my power is strongest when you are weak'[3] or as another version puts it – 'the less you have, the more you depend on Him'[4]. This seemed to be God's answer for the uncertainty and fear that we felt; it gave us the courage and reassurance we needed, reminding us that God is faithful and would be with us in whatever lay ahead.

We flew into Kenya in January 1979 where we had to wait for some weeks for the arrival of a VW Combi van, which was being shipped out from the UK. Finally we had news it had arrived at Mombasa. Going to collect it we visited our old head master, known affectionately as 'Pa Lavers'. He and his wife Pearl generously gave us a place to stay the night, and they offered to pray for us before we began our journey into Uganda.

Fear is defined by Wikipedia like this: *"Fear is an emotion induced by a threat perceived by living entities, which causes a change in brain and organ function and ultimately a change in behaviour, such as running away, hiding or freezing from traumatic events"*. And that

3   2 Corinthians 12:9 *Good News* Bible

4   2 Corinthians 12:9 *The Message*

describes exactly how Rob felt about taking his family into Idi Amin's war torn Uganda. We did believe that God had called us, and that it was right to be going to Kagando, but Rob in particular had an increasingly paralysing fear, fed by the many stories of hi-jackings and killings in Uganda, about what might lie ahead. It was real, and was beginning to interfere with good planning and decision-making. As Peter ("Pa") Lavers and his wife prayed in tongues over us, that fear was lifted from Rob. Never again in those challenging days that lay ahead did he feel that "running away, hiding or freezing" fear that had been threatening faith and progress. It was without doubt a miraculous intervention of the Holy Spirit. We remember that as Peter and Pearl finished praying, as recorded at the time in Jen's diary, "all three children suddenly woke up and started crying for no apparent reason – we felt the powerful presence of the Holy Spirit". We were to face some scary situations in the times ahead, but God was with us, and had shown in this practical way that He had answers to our needs.

Daily news bulletins of the political situation in Uganda continued to paint a disturbing and dangerous picture. However, in February things sounded more settled so we thought it would be safe to try and make our way over the border from Kenya. We piled three small children and all our belongings, including a paraffin fridge perched on the roof, into our van and set off on the first leg of our 1100-kilometre journey from Nairobi to Kagando. That very day, unbeknown to us, the Tanzanian army, which was 'liberating' Uganda from the tyranny of Idi Amin's regime, had reached an area just inside the Ugandan border and were bombing the very road we were to travel on. Driving towards Uganda unaware of what was happening, we reached Eldoret, 100 Kilometres from the Uganda border, where we planned to stay at the home of missionaries for the night. Arriving there, we were met with frantic messages warning us to go no further, but to return to Nairobi. As we turned back to Nairobi, next morning, we felt deeply disappointed, but immensely grateful not to be caught up in the fighting. Had we travelled just one day earlier things would have been very different. It was just one of the many times we saw God's miraculous planning and timing.

With the "liberation war" raging in Uganda, we were grateful to be offered a flat in which to stay at Kijabe, a large AIM station on the Eastern edge of the Great Rift Valley in Kenya, with a very busy hospital, school, and a great deal else going on. During those months of waiting in Kenya, Rob was able to work in the hospital as well as gaining invaluable experience in the community health work, visiting dispensaries in different parts of the country. Working with very experienced, knowledgeable and skilful missionary clinicians, this time was again God given, equipping Rob for the times that lay ahead when he would be on his own in the coming years. As a family, we looked forward to getting settled somewhere soon, but the time was well spent and we learnt many things, developed good friendships, and were further prepared for what lay ahead.

In May, when most of the fighting was over, and Idi Amin was fleeing for his life in the north of the country, it was felt that the situation was safe enough to try again to get into Uganda. This time however, Rob left his children and now eight-month pregnant wife in Nairobi, and left with Keith Waddell to make the first journey to Kagando since the start of the liberation war.

Setting out once again in a very heavily laden Volkswagen Combi, Keith and Rob crossed the border into Uganda. Everywhere there was evidence of the fierce battles that had taken place, with military vehicles and tanks littering the roads, and buildings that had been heavily shelled. The previously proud and bustling town of Mbarara, capital of the Ankole region of Uganda, was particularly badly affected. Driving through, it seemed as though every single building had been deliberately shelled leaving it looking like a ghost town. The streets were empty apart from a few wandering goats and the occasional chicken.

They lost count of the number of military roadblocks between Kampala and Kagando after counting twenty-five. Sometimes there were only a few hundred metres between them; their purpose, it seemed, had more to do with extracting bribes than a genuine concern about security. Police or soldiers, either from Tanzania, or Ugandans, who had joined the invading army, manned some. Other groups who set up roadblocks were disenchanted youths who were out to cause trouble after years of living in fear. Some of these appeared to be no more than teenagers; all carried loaded weapons, usually the old but lethal .303 rifles, frequently with little evidence that they knew how to use them safely. At nearly every roadblock, soldiers insisted on searching the heavily laden van, but eventually gave up in the absence of a bribe. The journey lasted a very long day.

Keith and Rob were very uncertain about what they would find at Kagando. There were no means of communication between Kagando and the outside world at that time, other than by word of mouth, and very few people were prepared to travel. Arriving just after dark, they were met with wonderful enthusiasm, and great hugs for the returning "Dr Keith". Incredibly, the hospital was safe, and functioning effectively under the leadership of Bonny Baluku, the manager. Medical treatments were very limited, but with a small supply of a simple range of anti-malarials, antibiotics, and a few other drugs, William, the medical assistant, and nurse Catherine, with their team of "nurse aids", had been able to care effectively for many patients.

There was no electricity, the generator having long since broken down; water was carried in jerry cans 400 metres up the hill from a small river, as the pump also had broken, and the water itself was heavily contaminated with every form of water borne disease. The house that we were to live in had mud walls, concrete floor, and a low corrugated iron roof with no ceiling. There was a front door that opened when you leaned against it (whether locked or not) and a back door made from weld mesh hanging on pieces of wire which served as hinges; there were no internal doors.

A few days later Rob drove back to Kampala and was able to make phone contact with Jen back in Nairobi, unsure if it was wise for them to be joining him soon. He advised that the family should stay in Nairobi until the situation improved further. After some discussion and slight pressure from Jen, it was decided that they should fly in a light aircraft to Entebbe, together with Lois Clark, the AIM nurse returning to Kagando after the war. They duly arrived the next day at Entebbe, and Rob was able to drive out onto the tarmac of this international airport to meet them. There were no commercial flights and no immigration or passport control to pass through. The airport was almost completely destroyed, and virtually deserted, in keeping with most of Entebbe, Kampala and the surrounding countryside.

Again, police and army roadblocks frequently interrupted the long journey, although they were already fewer in number compared to the previous week. After leaving the town of Mbarara, the road was blocked by a group of marching Tanzanian soldiers. One of them, who had a physique rather like that of Mohammed Ali, put his large hand through the window, grabbed Rob by the throat and shook him hard on being told that we had no cigarettes to give him.

There were difficulties, but we really enjoyed being back in Uganda, with its lush vegetation, friendly people and the incredibly beautiful view that opens up as one comes to the edge of the rift valley driving west. The valley floor goes through the Queen Elizabeth game park and across the Kazinga Channel, which connects Lake George to Lake Edward and then rises sharply as the Rwenzori Mountains beyond. The bridge crossing the channel once spanned the River Thames but it was shipped out to Uganda in the 1950's when it became redundant at its original UK site. A notice describing its origins still marks this strategic bridge. Remarkably, it has remained intact for sixty years or more, withstanding the pounding of army tanks, overladen trucks and buses, and somehow avoiding the attention of those who could have wrought havoc by destroying the bridge during periods of conflict.

We were warmly welcomed to Kagando and our basic little house quickly became 'home'. We were privileged to experience, from the start, the warm and genuine hospitality of the Bakonzo people, who were endlessly forgiving of our cultural blunders. We knew that we were there as guests, but in retrospect we can see how much we took for granted, and how insensitive we must have seemed to our hosts. We appreciated their kindness very much as communication with the outside world was very sparse.

The children coped remarkably well with life in a war zone, and were not unduly perturbed by the sight of soldiers with guns, burnt out tanks and bombed buildings, with frequent gunfire at night. They settled well into the new home and environment with the daily routine of 'going to school' in a little trailer tent found near the house, with Mum being the teacher during those 'school hours'. Rob was immediately immersed in the busyness of the hospital, and the daily routines were soon established.

After arrival at Kagando there was just over a month in which to prepare for the birth of the new baby. We tried to be ready for whatever circumstances might prevail when labour started; we set aside two spare mantles with a supply of kerosene for the pressure lamp in case the birth happened at night. We had a sterile "delivery pack" to hand, and made sure that there was a 'jerry can' full of water.

Life was full, and there was no time to worry about what could go wrong… But God was good, and we were so grateful that in the end Stephen arrived in daylight and without complications. Getting the news out to our families in the UK was a challenge and something we had tried to prepare for. We tried, but failed to set up two-way radio communication; the nearest working telephone was in Kampala, 400 kilometres away, and post took many weeks. The best we could do was to write two letters with the news of Stephen's birth, one sent by courier (the driver of a Uganda Protestant Medical Bureau truck, who had brought emergency medical supplies for the hospital), and the other posted in Kasese, 50 kilometres away, along with a telegram. The telegram took the longest to arrive, at 6 weeks!

Philip, Ruth, Stephen and Esther. Life was fun and free.

In retrospect, now with grandchildren of our own, we realise how tough that must have been for our families – but we felt so blessed that our families trusted God, and also trusted us. Ruth, Philip and Esther took all these changes very calmly, and doted on their little brother – who caused quite a stir amongst the local people as he was the first white baby to have been born there for many years. Stephen was later baptised in the local Church of Uganda church, St John's Church, Kisinga.

After three years of home schooling, we thought that Ruth and Philip needed more social contact with their peers. So we reluctantly made the tough decision to send them to the same boarding school, St Andrews, Turi, that we had both attended as children in Kenya. They did well, and Ruth was made head girl in her final year.

We found the separation much harder as parents than we had as children! With no means of communication, we often did not receive their weekly letters from the time we left them at school until we next visited them at half term; each trip to the school was a 960 kilometre, two-day road journey with an uncertain border crossing each way.

Although the separation was painful, as a family we had some wonderful holidays together, visiting places we would not otherwise have gone to. One memorable time was staying with Rob's brother, Chris, in a remote part of Western Kenya. He was working as a missionary, also under TEAR Fund, as an agriculturalist, helping Masai tribesmen to improve the management of their precious cattle, and equally precious grazing land. It was very wild with few tracks, but it reminded us in some ways of what the Garden of Eden must have been like. With wild animals – buck, leopards, wonderful birds – roaming freely, and living alongside the nomadic Masai, who were finding it increasingly hard to find grazing land for their cattle.

Chris started his work among them by building a church, then a home for the church pastor. All this time he lived in a tent, keeping his supplies in a temporary round metal hut. Once he had built the church and pastor's home, he built a home for himself. He planned to marry Jenny, his fiancée back in the UK, and they were then going to serve there at Masarura together. They duly married in the UK, but tragedy struck before their return; a speeding motorcyclist struck Jenny when she was cycling with Chris, and she died. Chris never returned to the home he had built.

Before this tragedy, on an occasion when we were staying with Chris, we stopped with him to have a picnic at a spectacular spot overlooking the Masai Mara game park. As we enjoyed the picnic and the view we were suddenly interrupted by the sound of lions roaring close by. The two men, Chris and Rob, shielded the family for the 100 metres back to the car. There were buffalo nearby, but there was no sign of the lion. However, as we started to drive off, we heard the lions' roar again. Driving off the track through long grass in the direction from which we had heard the roar, we found the lions – in a cage! We had inadvertently stumbled on the film set of a company making the film 'Out of Africa'! We met members of the film making team who were welcoming and friendly. When we later saw the film, we recognised our picnic spot – used in the final scene where the "hero" was buried!

After Ruth and Philip had started boarding school, Esther and Stephen then took their turn in the little schoolroom, although they easily became distracted by all the activity going on around them. Stephen specially longed to join the workman in slashing the grass, watching them kill a snake, going to the river in the tractor to collect stones or just digging holes. They used to call him 'Bwana Kazi', a Swahili phrase meaning "Mr Work", in respect for all his hard work! He could often be seen at the age of four or five, working away with the workmen, sweating profusely in the heat. One of Esther's favourite pastimes was to put on a mask and spend hours in the operating theatre watching her father doing all sorts of complex surgical procedures! When at home, all the children made good friends with their Ugandan neighbours, often playing in their homes for hours at a time. Life was fun and free for them. Children were and are treasured in that culture, and we never felt threatened – our children or ourselves – by our wonderful hospitable neighbours.

CHAPTER FOUR

Hospital & medical work

"The First Duty of Love is to Listen" [1]

In the hospital, sometimes working as the only doctor there, Rob often felt overwhelmed at the prospect of what needed to be done, and he developed an enormous respect for others, particularly Dr Keith Waddell, who had coped alone for so long, so well. The medical work was a constant learning process, often fascinating, constantly demanding, sometimes frightening. The range of disease encountered at Kagando was huge.

Emergencies at night were not uncommon – most frequently obstetric. But some were quite dramatic. Very memorably, on three successive nights, patients were brought in with serious injuries from three different wild animals. The first night a man was brought in who had been bitten by a hippopotamus in Lake Edward, 30 kilometres away. Typically terribly dirty crush injuries, such bites on a limb could often only be managed by limb amputation, with a view to saving the patient's life. This was no exception; wound debridement and cleaning were obviously inadequate, and so his leg was amputated. But he survived.

The next night a woman was brought in very late. The story was that she had got up, and gone out of her home, a simple mud walled, thatched roof house, to use

1   Paul Tillich

49

the toilet. Attacked by a lion, which had started to drag her away by her head, she screamed and alerted others who came running and scared the lion away. Amazingly still alive, she was actually suffering only relatively minor injury considering the attack – but that injury was the loss of almost her whole scalp. Her relatives had managed to rescue some of the scalp, and brought it along with her. She too survived, and after long and repeated skin grafts was eventually able to go home, but with scalp that no longer bore hair for the most part.

On the third night, another injury, another wild animal. This time it was a man who, with others, had been trying to kill an elephant with spears. Gaining the upper hand, the elephant had picked him up and thrown him down on the ground. He arrived at Kagando with an acutely painful, distended abdomen, but amazingly no broken bones. There was no X-ray at that time, and ultrasound was yet to find its way into normal medical practice anywhere, yet alone in Uganda. So performing an exploratory operation – opening him up to discover what was wrong – was the only way to find out what

Asbestos huts under the trees, which were the hospital wards.

injuries he had. Inside he had some torn tissues, and free blood, but otherwise nothing very major. He too survived, but developed accumulations of fluid (a "pseudo cyst") that had to be drained off from time to time afterwards.

But the great majority of the hospital's work was treating diseases very common to that area; malaria in particular was, and remains, extremely common. It was easy to understand from the perspective of Kagando how malaria can kill a million people worldwide every year. Tuberculosis in all its forms, with all its complications, was common. Childhood illnesses, particularly malaria, hookworm, severe anaemia, measles, meningitis and pneumonia were seen regularly in the outpatients department. Anthrax, now rarely seen in Western Europe, and more associated with threatened biomedical warfare, was endemic in an area near to Kagando. Often there were injuries linked with the war and several times Rob had to operate with a textbook propped up beside him, or with someone holding it, and turning to the appropriate page.

There was no alternative hospital to which patients could go; those who could not be treated at Kagando could not be transferred anywhere else, because of the cost and difficulty of transport, and the breakdown of government run medical services. So it was rare for patients to be transferred.

From the time of the AIM tech team visit and their successful repair of the electricity supplies, the generator ran for three hours every evening, from nightfall at 7.00pm to 10.00pm, and during some of the times when the operating theatre was in use, giving us light in some of the staff houses and the hospital. Operating lights in the hospital operating theatre were in the form of two car headlight units installed at either end of a silver lined hardboard frame that also housed four strip lights. For operating, it was therefore ideal that both the mains strip lights, and the adjustable battery powered car headlight units were working, but one or the other was just adequate for emergencies. A small portable generator was also used for emergencies at night. Whenever the main generator was running we tried to make sure that car batteries in the operating theatre, and in our home, were being charged – these then provided light for surgery by powering two car headlight units in the operating theatre, and for reading or studying by means of twelve volt bulbs in our home.

We had to watch every bit of fuel – whenever a vehicle or a generator was started up it had to be used as efficiently as possible; we saved up trips to Kasese until they had to be made, and as much in the way of different business as possible could be achieved in the one trip. One "additional thing" that could be achieved in the drive to Kasese was once again charging those twelve-volt batteries. Conveniently, you could fit an additional battery into the rear engine compartment of those old Volkswagen Combis. So, a second battery was always wired up in the battery compartment when the Combi was used to make a trip – and was then fully charged for the operating theatre light.

This battery charging arrangement worked well, except on one occasion. On this occasion, half way through the 50 Km trip into Kasese, the Combi suddenly stopped. Getting out to investigate we found smoke coming from the engine compartment at the back; the lead charging the extra battery had shorted, and started a fire. The car had stopped because the plastic petrol pipe supplying fuel to the engine had melted and broken, and petrol was pouring out of the pipe. Miraculously, in spite of the shorting cable, the heat and the smoke, the petrol had not ignited – we could not understand why or how disaster had been avoided with this lethal mix of burning and leaking petrol. But it had, and we stopped to thank God once again for His extraordinary protection.

Supplies for the hospital were in short supply. The bulk of the basic medicines needed to treat common diseases such as Malaria, Tuberculosis, Meningitis and anaemia were bought from the Government, through the Uganda Protestant Medical Bureau. Other supplies were sent in parcels from the USA and the UK. Everything had to be carefully accounted for, and used in the most economical way possible. Keith Waddell taught Rob many of the techniques, which he had developed, such as that for anaesthesia. He showed how he was able to use one vial of injection to last not just for the one intended patient, but could be divided up and made to serve four patients. Spinal anaesthesia could be achieved very economically by purchasing Procaine powder in bulk. This was then weighed and divided up into 100mg amounts; these were bottled and sterilized separately. Spinal Anaesthesia could be achieved by putting a needle into a patient's spine, withdrawing one millilitre of the spinal fluid, mixing it with 100mg of Procaine, and re injecting it into the patient's spine. The cost of the procedure, instead of being several pounds, was just a few Pence. For suturing, we used nylon fishing line, cut into lengths, threaded onto re usable needles, and sterilized.

It was difficult to get alcohol to make up skin cleaning solutions. So Rob would send a member of staff out to buy a few litres of "Waragi", the locally distilled gin. This was high concentration alcohol, and was effective used with iodine in making up topical sterilizing solution. But we tried to be careful not to be seen to support the "Waragi" industry, because of the tragic damage done by alcohol in the community.

Treatment by witch doctors included the very prevalent practices of "Obulho", and "Ebiino". When a patient complained of a persistent cough, the witch doctor taught that it was necessary to cut out the small area of breast tissue under their nipple ("Obulho"); so they did this, without anaesthetic, and with dirty instruments. When a child suffered from diarrhoea and vomiting, it was felt the best treatment was to remove the canine teeth ("Ebiino"), even before they had erupted through the gum – again without anaesthetic or clean instruments.

Patients with fever would have multiple superficial incisions on the skin – this was to release the evil spirits causing the fever. Newborn infants, their parents were told, should have their umbilical stumps covered in dung. Other "treatments" included the use of herbs; some of which were undoubtedly powerful. The hospital constantly had to pick up the pieces and treat the damage

Inside the asbestos hut wards it was dark and crowded, but they served their purpose at the time.

caused by these treatments – the infection, abscesses and septicaemia caused by Obulho and Ebino, and the neonatal tetanus caused by the practice of putting dung on the umbilicus resulted in much suffering, long term disfigurement and disability or even death.

Patients with bone fractures often seemed to go to the witch doctor before coming to the hospital because of a very strong belief in the power of witch doctors to heal broken bones. Visiting a witch doctor with a fractured limb, a patient first had to pay a large fee. They would then have makeshift splints applied to their limb, and were told to return home. The sign that the treatment was successful would be proved by the fact that at a particular time (and the witch doctor would be precise about this) the patient would experience very severe pain in the area of their fracture. And patients testified that, exactly as predicted, so they had experienced. No wonder their belief in the witch doctor was reinforced. Patients would also be told to return to the healer at regular intervals; he or she would remove the splint from the limb, manipulate the fracture without any anaesthetic and then replace the splint.

In addition to the witch doctors, there were other traditional healers in the communities around Kagando. Some of their treatments were helpful, such as an agent obtained from particular roots, which are effective in reducing fever, and relieving discomfort. Others are highly dangerous, like the oxytocic agents[2] used in pregnant mothers. Tragically, these could cause powerful sustained contractions of the mother's uterus, risking the baby's life,

2   Oxytocic agents. Chemicals which act in the same way as Oxytocin, a natural hormone in women which causes the Uterus (womb) to contract.

and resulting in impacted labour, with all its possible risks. These oxytocic agents are also used to induce illegal abortions.

One day, a teenager was admitted to Kagando suffering the consequences of an illegal attempt at inducing abortion on her five-month foetus. Oxytocic agents derived from the roots of locally grown herbs had been administered and, to increase their effect, bands had been tied around her body. These bands were applied in a way to put great pressure on her abdomen, including her uterus. After many hours she was brought to the hospital in a state of severe shock. Her baby was dead. But the combination of her pregnancy, the treatments administered to her, and the severe pressure applied to her abdomen had caused a complete blockage of the main arteries that supplied her legs. Desperate attempts were made with surgery to see if these blockages could be cleared – but they were very extensive, surgery failed, and she died.

The witch doctors and traditional healers had historically seen the hospital as competition, threatening their livelihoods. As people's trust in the hospital grew, with increasing experience of caring, successful treatment, the witch doctors abandoned their outright opposition, and started to employ other tactics. The hospital's treatment, they declared, would only work if patients first sought the witchdoctors' treatment and blessing. And this treatment and "blessing" was expensive. So the witch doctors, because of the deeply, strongly held beliefs in the powers wielded by these practitioners, were able to make a great deal of money. This was frequently and tragically at the expense of seriously ill patients who really could not afford to pay anything.

CHAPTER FIVE

Rwenzururu United Kingdom

*"As long as you are tangled in wrong and revenge,
blow and counterblow, aggression and defence,
you will be constantly drawn into fresh wrong...
Only forgiveness frees us from the injustice
of others."* [1]

The Bakonzo people have had many struggles over the past 150 years – against the Batoro (the tribe to the north), the British and Belgian colonists as well as the post independent Ugandan governments. The area was a classic example of the way Western nations carved up parts of traditional Africa without heed to the claims of less vocal peoples. Their mountain region was simply split down the middle by the 1910 Anglo Belgian agreement that the Congo-Nile watershed would be the boundary between Congo and Uganda. This left one fifth of the tribe in Uganda and the rest in Congo, both with the same traditions and speaking essentially the same language

The Bakonzo people were despised by many of the Batoro, particularly as they regarded them as being backward, and for being related to the mountain pygmies.

In 1921 three Bakonzo men whose names were Nyamutswa, Kapolya and Tibamwenda mobilised their

---

1   Roamano Guardini, theologian

tribe to rebel against the Batoro, but they were quickly caught and killed. A monument, built in their honour, stands in the grounds of Kagando Primary School at the place where they were buried. The Bakonzo people planted a tree in memory of these three men, whose families still live in the area. This monument serves also as a reminder of the central place that Kagando has in the history of the Bakonzo tribe. It would be several decades after the men were killed before the Bakonzo would make another attempt to gain independence from the Batoro

But, in the 1950s the Bakonzo people again requested a separation from the Toro kingdom, but this was refused by the colonial authorities.

The dispute continued, and came to a head in 1962 when the Bakonzo received no mention in the Ugandan independence constitution. As a result, a part of the tribe broke away and declared itself independent from the rest of Uganda, calling themselves the Rwenzururu United Kingdom, under the leadership of Isaya Mukirane. He had been a teacher, working in Bundibugyo in the northern part of the Bakonzo kingdom before he was elected to the Toro parliament. However, feeling aggrieved because the Bakonzo request had been ignored, he gathered a significant group from the tribe to rebel and join him in the mountains.

President Obote sent in troops to 'deal with' this breakaway group, but all attempts failed. Later on Idi Amin and the presidents who followed him sent their armies into the mountains, but they were all unable to subdue the members of this movement, who were later led by King Charles Wesley Mumbere Irema Ngoma, the son of the original king.

In 1979 after the overthrow of Idi Amin, the Rwenzururu re-established their movement, obtaining a large store of weapons and other equipment following the liberation war, as well as receiving support from abroad. Very early one morning long before daybreak, Rob witnessed a ten-ton lorry full of new looking rifles travelling past the hospital with no lights, moving towards the mountain. The Rwenzururu had found some way to obtain these, even though they could afford very little else.

This posed a real threat to the local Bakonzo people, and had an enormous impact on Kagando. It was caught between this small but passionate, well-armed group and central government. Both sides were equally determined to succeed in their mission, but were unable to carry it out. Each claimed that the hospital was in their territory and therefore must abide by their rules and not treat the soldiers of the opposing side. The local people had to pay taxes to the Ugandan Government as well as to the Rwenzururu movement.

The Rwenzori mountain range was a no go area for all outsiders at this time, but in 1980 a correspondent from the Observer, Nick Worrall, got permission to go into the mountains to visit the King. After he had been checked and searched for eight hours by two Rwenzururu "cabinet ministers", he received permission to walk up 1,000 metres through dense vegetation to meet the King, out in the open and far from his 'palace'. He was introduced to the members of the cabinet but the King explained that they were not politicians. He said 'I was appointed by God and they are appointed by me. There are no politics in Rwenzururu'. He described how his people, friendless and with no outside assistance, had held off the entire world and were not recognised by United Nations or the Commonwealth in spite of his requests that they should be seen as an independent kingdom.

There is a local saying, which goes: 'When the elephant and the hippo fight it is the grass that suffers'[2]. This was certainly true for Kagando and the people living around there at that time. We witnessed some of the tragic consequences of patients who had been beaten, raped and suffered loss of their hands, cut by one or other of the two warring sides because they had had the temerity to try to hold onto their possessions. At Kagando, we housed people who were too frightened to stay in their own homes. We saw and treated those who had been injured, and heard of sporadic loss of life of innocent people caught in the fighting.

On one occasion when he was in Kampala, Rob happened to meet a BBC news reporter from the UK and told him of all that was going on in the West. The correspondent just had two questions. 'Is there a massacre?' and 'Can I get there and back in a day?' The negative answers to both questions meant that he was not interested, and the outside world still would have little knowledge of what was going on.

Gradually we gained the trust of the Rwenzeruru, and used to receive letters from the King or one of his ministers requesting treatment for an illness in one of them. Summoned up into the mountain and carrying basic medication we would meet the king and his bodyguard. We took the stand, that as a hospital we treated all patients equally, regardless of racial, tribal or religious background, and so we were able to establish a good

---

2   Old Lhukonzo saying

working relationship with both the Rwenzururu and the national government, both of whom generally supported Kagando.

During that time when travel and communication was difficult and land was cheap, it was suggested that we might build an airstrip near the hospital. The Rwenzururu supported the idea and AIM-Air pilots who checked out the site thought it was feasible. However, in the end it was turned down by Central Government who were concerned about security.

Looking back to those turbulent days from the present time, with peace with the Rwenzururu apparently secure, and the local population growing rapidly, it seems hard to picture the tensions that existed during the height of the troubles between the movement in the mountains and central Government. Sadly, tensions do still exist below the surface, as demonstrated by the deaths of seventy people early in 2014. These recent clashes appear to have come about as a result of growing resentment over the use of land considered to belong to the Rwenzururu Kingdom. At the height of the troubles we were very conscious of God's hand over the situation at Kagando. We prayed daily for His protection, and do believe that Kagando's safety then, and still remains, an answer to prayer. "For he will command his angels concerning you to guard you in all your ways; they will lift you up in their hands, so that you will not strike your foot against a stone…"[3]

In the mid eighties President Obote negotiated a settlement in which the Rwenzururu agreed to abandon their goal of secession in exchange for a degree of autonomy. The King was offered economic benefits and

---

3   Psalm 91:11,12

educational scholarships in return for a peaceful end to the years of turbulence and bloodshed.

Yoweri Museveni, who became President of Uganda in 1986, agreed to reinstate all the kingdoms for the tribes who wanted a cultural leader. So after an extended period of time abroad, Irema Ngoma was able to return to Uganda. He now lives in Kasese protected by his bodyguard, which is provided by central government.

Tribal kings, it is hoped, will uphold cultural values and mobilise the local people in social economic development, such as health, education and agriculture, and have potential to bring about a united purpose. Remarkably, those who perpetrated the killings in 2014, after acknowledging their guilt and seeking forgiveness, received a pardon. The prayer of those in leadership in the church, and at Kagando, is that this act of statesmanship might be used to defuse tensions, and secure peace for the future. "If everyone followed the 'eye for an eye' principle of justice, the whole world would be blind"...[4]

---

4   Mahatma Ghandi

CHAPTER SIX

"Do you remember that night?" Rwenzururu soldier

'Don't be afraid! Stand your ground and you will see what the Lord your God will do" [1]

"Dokita! Dokita! Dokita"![2] The nurse who had just run up the 200 metre slope from the hospital to our home was panting hard, and could hardly get the words out. In the pitch black of the night we couldn't see her face, but the fear in her cry was unmistakeable. "Come quickly… soldiers…!"

Emergencies in the hospital aren't uncommon and are often the result of serious complications in childbirth. One gets used to the frantic pounding at the door and the panting voice calling, "Dokita, dokita[2], … flat baby, flat baby" – meaning a child just born is not responding as expected, or simply not breathing at all. The calls are not false alarms and it became routine to throw on some clothes and sprint down the hill at all hours of the day and night.

---

1   Exodus 14:13

2   "Dokita" was how the Ugandan nurses' pronunciation of the word "Doctor" sounded, especially when they were short of breath and anxious. Their command of English was good. We were humbled and ashamed that our command of their language, Lhukonzo, was, and remains, so poor.

On this occasion there was something different about the call. The night was the same – typical of what happens in this part of Africa; on the equator, at about three and a half thousand feet above sea level, it never gets really cold, but the heat of the day is replaced by a gentle breeze off the Ruwenzori mountains. There was the sound of crickets, more obvious once the hospital generator had been turned off at 10.00 pm by a night watchman. In the distance a drumbeat shared messages across the hills and valleys – this was well before the days of mobile phones. The sounds of funerals were frequent, as people drummed and danced to appease the spirits. Popular belief was that these spirits would punish the one who had died, as well as the surviving relatives unless they were appeased by the all night vigils, accompanied by drumming and dancing.

This call was frantic. The terror in the nurse's words, "Come quickly – soldiers", was tangible and infectious. The "flight or fight" symptoms resulting from a sharp increase in blood adrenalin levels – the dry mouth and rapid pulse – were very strong as Rob ran down the hill, not at all sure what he was going to find.

The patient had been brought into "the doctors' office", a room adjacent to the operating theatre. This was the normal place for assessing emergencies before deciding on a plan of action. Once the initial assessment was done, whatever treatment was believed to be the best way to manage a particular problem was started. He was a fit looking young man, with a strong, muscular body. But he was lying helpless on the makeshift stretcher, made from two poles connected by elephant grass, bound together with banana fibre, and carried by a group of about six other young men. Each of the young men carried a Kalashnikov rifle and the atmosphere was very tense. The light, provided by kerosene lanterns, was limited, and the smell of "waragi" (gin, distilled from banana juice) was strong.

The message being translated to Rob was becoming clearer. The group were soldiers of the Rwenzururu United Kingdom. Their mission that night was not clear, but they may have been engaged in retribution against people they suspected of being collaborators with the Ugandan government. Whatever it was, things had not gone as planned, and their comrade, lying on the stretcher, had been injured. Apparently knifed in the back, he was now paraplegic, with no use or feeling in his legs from the waist down.

Rob became the uncomfortable centre of attention as men pointed their guns at him, and insisted that he "cure their comrade" immediately. From a medical perspective it quickly became obvious that there was no prospect of a rapid cure, indeed little prospect of any recovery at all, the knife in his back having almost certainly cut through much of his spinal cord. The threatened use of those Kalashnikov rifles seemed very real and imminent. Rob felt fearful and very much alone, as he was the only doctor at Kagando at the time.

A notice at the entrance to the hospital compound which said "no firearms in the hospital" gave Rob the courage to state that he would not even look at, let alone seek to cure the patient until all the guns were out of the hospital compound. Tension rose, and there was a silence which seemed to last a long time before finally, one of the men started to leave the room, going out into the darkness. As the last of them left, there was a deafening volley of shots – they were defiantly shooting into the air before leaving. Hearing the shots back at the house, Jen feared that Rob might well have been shot.

Rob got the wounded soldier onto an examination couch, and tried to assess the extent of the injury. The hospital's means of investigation at that time did not include X-rays, Ultrasound, or any other way to image what was under the skin, and clinicians had to rely on what could be found on physical examination. It seemed as bad as it had first appeared; the wounded man had only minimal sensation below the waist, with no ability to move his legs at all. The best that could be done was to clean and dress the wound in his back, insert a urinary catheter, and provide nursing care while waiting to see to what extent he might recover.

The next morning, Kagando had a problem. The paraplegic soldier remained an inpatient, fed and cared for by the hospital staff (patients normally had their own relatives or friends to provide food and personal care). This soldier's home was about sixty kilometres north of Kagando, and his family did not dare appear because of fear of arrest by the Ugandan army... inevitably, the Ugandan authorities heard about this Rwenzururu soldier, receiving inpatient care at Kagando. They demanded that the hospital hand him over to the authorities, to which the hospital was able to reply, rightly, that he was too seriously injured to leave hospital at that time. Once again, stalemate existed. To have handed him over to the authorities would have brought immediate and violent retribution from the Rwenzururu; to refuse to hand him over risked condemnation by the authorities, and the possibility of sanctions being applied – such as withdrawal of our visas.

Time was on our side. The Rwenzururu soldier did well, and regained a tiny bit of sensation in his legs. With the passage of time, the local Ugandan authorities forgot about the soldier, and one day Keith took him by car back to his home area, and delivered him to his family.

Fast forward in time, thirty-two years later, and Irema Ngoma Charles Wesley, his army disbanded, but now re-instated officially as King of the Rwenzururu people by President Museveni, is living in a modest palace in Kasese. He has constitutional rights under the Ugandan government to represent the Rwenzururu people. We were invited to visit the King in 2012, and found him looking almost unchanged from our mountainside meetings more than thirty years before. As we talked, he asked, "Do you remember Dennis on the night he came to Kagando?" The name was not familiar, but it became clear that Dennis was the man brought into the hospital, paralyzed by a knife wound to his back in 1979. Amazingly, he is not only still alive, but has slowly recovered to the point that he can now walk a little, with some assistance!

CHAPTER SEVEN

Team Players
AIM tech lorry

The Lord's unfailing love and mercy still continue,
fresh as the morning, as sure as the sunrise [1]

Exactly a week after Stephen was born, Kagando received an incalculable blessing and, again, the timing was extraordinary.

It was just after the end of the day's work in the hospital, shadows had lengthened, and the characteristically rapid change from day to night of the tropics was soon to come. The sound of a heavily laden lorry making its way up the hill to the houses behind the hospital brought everyone out to see what was coming. It was a heavy duty, ex German military truck, the kind that will go anywhere, and could run on almost whatever fuel you chose – from petrol, diesel, kerosene to cooking oil. It was driven by a branch of Africa Inland Mission, called AIM tech. In the truck were pioneer American AIM missionaries, Dr Jim Propst, then in his 70's, his son John and his wife Pam, and a Canadian colleague, Ray Jealouse, along with an armed guard who had helped them through the roadblocks. The truck was packed with spares, cable, roofing sheets, guttering, pipe and everything else that was needed to revitalise Kagando, as well as drums of fuel and sacks of food.

---

1   Lamentations 3:23

It was a miracle in itself that they had driven the 1100 kilometres from Nairobi, arriving safely with all the goods intact. They had been delayed a week by political unrest in Kampala otherwise they would have arrived 3 hours after our baby did! By the following week we were much more ready to entertain and help them with all the sorting out that was needed.

They were our first visitors and were such an encouragement in every way. By the time they finished all the work a few weeks later, the generator and water pumps were working, the compound had been re wired, and electrical fittings, pipes, taps, roofs, guttering, kerosene operated sterilizers were all repaired and functioning as they should. What a transformation!

We now had running water at strategic points in the hospital, and in our homes, lights that you could switch on instead of fiddling around with matches and kerosene lanterns, or "Tilley pressure lamps". Of course the lanterns were still needed in the hours of darkness for the hospital wards, and staff got into the routine of lighting them up before the generator was switched off.

From that time on the generator ran for three hours every evening, from nightfall at 7.00pm to 10.00pm, and during some of the times when the operating theatre was in use, giving us light in the staff houses and the hospital. A small portable generator was also used for emergencies at night.

The AIM tech team also worked on the diesel pump on the riverbank below the hospital. John Mattison, a missionary engineer with CMS, and based in Kampala, had previously also worked successfully on this old but highly effective single cylinder Lister diesel, so there was not much that was needed to get it going. From then on it pumped water 500 metres up the hill to an area above the compound, where the tank from a crashed petrol tanker, abandoned on the roadside, acted as the reservoir for all the water needs of the hospital and staff houses.

The water pumped from the river was almost untreated; at best it came through a simple sand filter in the river bed[2], to remove the worst of the dirt only. We tried to improve the quality of the water taken from the tank by putting a better sand filter in the tank outlet – but it remained simple, and it was essential to treat or boil this water before drinking it. One day this filter in the outlet to the tank became blocked. The only way to clear it was to dive into the full tank and manually remove the blockage. So Rob duly climbed in and dived down to try to sort out the problem; it was successful, but he ended up catching cholera from the contaminated water. He spent that night on the outdoor long drop toilet, pouring from both ends, but taking in water, salt and sugar as fast as, or faster than it came out, and he felt better the next morning...

2   http://www.who.int/water_sanitation_health/
    publications/ssf/en/

CHAPTER EIGHT

Road Blocks

Do not be afraid, I am with you.... when you pass
through deep waters, I will be with you...
You are precious to me [1]

Where two or three are gathered together in Jesus'
Name, there is a mess! [2]

Any form of travel was hazardous and unpredictable. Different friends shared their stories and experiences with us. One story involved two single missionary ladies with a child, who were stopped at a roadblock near the Owen Falls Dam at Jinja. Accused of crossing the roadblock "line", they were removed from their vehicle, beaten up and then all four tyres were shot. Another friend was forced to strip down to his underpants, and made to run along the road with no shoes on. A couple with their toddler had to lie on the road and were told they were about to be shot until the soldiers suddenly realised just in time that these were not the people they were looking for.

For our family too, roadblocks played a big part of our lives whenever we were travelling. Some roadblocks were frightening with guns thrust through the windows

---

1   Isaiah 43:2,4

2   George Verwer, Director of *Operation Mobilisation*

and soldiers demanding our identity, money or cigarettes. Some were tedious when soldiers wanted a bribe or had nothing better to do than take up their time by searching through all our belongings.

Once we saw the funny side later when the soldier became more and more irritated by our lack of response after asking to see our "transport". Failing to satisfy him by showing him the vehicle in which we were travelling, we finally realised he was asking to see our "passports" which we duly showed him. He glanced at them upside down, and waved us on. Another time when our belongings were being checked, the soldiers saw Rob's violin case. Instantly suspicious, they demanded to see what was inside. After playing them a tune, the tension eased, and we were allowed to drive on.

Occasionally there were friendly faces that were distracted by white children and they managed to make a joke with them. We thanked God every time for His protection and were so grateful that the children did not suffer physically or emotionally by these contacts with sometimes unscrupulous, greedy and rude groups of people.

This protection seemed miraculous on many occasions. To share "father" time together, relieve Jen slightly in her unending work of home and childcare, hostess to the many visitors and hospital cashier, Rob would sometimes take one or other of the children away on a trip. This time it was Philip's turn. Aged 8 years old, he was a wonderful mixture of enthusiasm and inquisitiveness, and coped incredibly well with a tedious journey to Kampala, even more tedious waiting at offices and warehouses as they did paperwork and got hospital supplies.

On the return journey, the Combi packed absolutely full with boxes of supplies, leaving just the driver's seat and a small area beside it for Phil, they got to within twenty five kilometres of home. Daring to think of the clean water, meal and beds that waited for them back at home, they just had two more roadblocks to negotiate at the Kazinga Channel crossing. The first was straightforward, and the soldiers waved them through. Three quarters of a mile further, on the other side of the village of Katunguru, they met with problems. The soldier there, possibly "high" on drugs, certainly sensing a massive treasure trove in the overladen vehicle, harangued, shouted, abused and threatened. Probably trying to provoke a reaction that would give him an excuse to attack Rob and Phil, or possessing just enough uncertainty in his mind as to whether he could get away with disposing of them and stealing the vehicle – it was impossible to tell. Night fell during the hour or so that he spent verbally attacking in this way. Finally, as a saloon car came up behind (rare at that time of the evening), he suddenly allowed them to go. Rob was shaking and exhausted as they drove into the dark. The real miracle, however, was Philip. Throughout what could have been a terrifying experience for him he had been absorbed in playing a game with toy cars on the floor at the front of the van. As they drove off he looked up at Rob and said "Dad, that was a long road block, wasn't it?" It seemed such a miracle that Philip was kept safe from what could have been a painful and difficult memory.

We all got used to scanning the road ahead as we drove, and the first person to see something suspicious, such as a pile of clothes, or a stick beside the road, would call out and we would quickly hide the cassette player that we used for playing children's songs, and start to prepare mentally for what was always an unpredictable encounter. A favourite ploy by the soldiers manning the blocks was to accuse the driver of "ignoring the road block" – this might involve the front wheel of the car just passing the line of the block – which would be marked by any random article. This accusation was then used to add pressure to requests for a bribe or favour, such as cigarettes. With God's help we never handed over money (but often paid in frustration with the delays); we also had no cigarettes. But we did often try to form some kind of relationship with those manning the blocks; many were very young, most were obviously feeling insecure, and hardly any had access to medical care – and Rob did exploit that occasionally, offering simple treatments for obvious health problems. We also always carried leaflets, which summarised the Christian gospel of love, mercy and reconciliation, and gave them to those manning the roadblocks. Often they were interested, and always they were spiritually hungry people. We tried to consciously see these men, and very occasionally women, through Jesus' eyes. What would Jesus see, looking at this insecure, often frightened, person? We realised that it was their lack of faith in a loving God that was the root of their fear, and their feelings of insecurity that led them to behave in what was sometimes such an irrational way.

Years later, two days after our eventual return to the UK, our youngest son commented 'Dad, we haven't had any roadblocks for a long time'. And then early one morning, a few weeks later, we realised that the house was very quiet. Looking out of the window we saw that all four of our children had set up a roadblock in our very middle class housing estate in Lindfield, and were asking to see the passports of all the unsuspecting people who were trying to go by! We quietly slipped away, and pretended the children were nothing to do with us...

There were many challenges to working at Kagando that were 'roadblocks' to progress. Work in the hospital was busy and demanding. There were frequent night calls, sometimes to a sick patient on the ward, others to a crying baby at home. There was always more to do than the time or resources with which to do it, and tiredness built up. The one thing that seemed to work well in Uganda at that time was information gathering by the security services. A local MP, Hon Amon Bazira, was very involved in the running of the security services, and we were sometimes surprised at how much was known about the movements of ourselves, and other expatriates working at Kagando. We were often very aware of the spiritual battle there at Kagando, and were reminded that we "struggle ...not against flesh and blood, but against the rulers, against the authorities, against the powers of this dark world and against the spiritual forces of evil in the heavenly realms"[3].

But one of the greatest difficulties was that of day-to-day relationships with fellow workers. We were privileged to work with wonderful women and men of God, who were seeking to serve God in what they were doing, and making great sacrifices to be there at Kagando. But we were all strong personalities with clear views about what should be done and how. There was little structure at that time that would give security or clarity over leadership. Many missionaries around the world face great tensions, whether single or as married couples, as they have to live

3   Ephesians 6:12

and work and pray together in small compounds. Mission societies and non-Governmental organisations of the twenty first century are far more aware of the psychological pressures facing workers in isolated circumstances. Looking back at our childhood experiences in mission situations, we were aware that our parents had faced similar situations. Even the apostles in the Bible had their differences![4]

In the morning prayers, which were held before work in the hospital every day, different people took turns to give a short talk. Rob still remembers one day when Lois Clark, our nurse colleague, was speaking. She was talking about eternity, using the words of St Paul: "Live in harmony with one another"[5]. She reminded us clearly that as Christians we will all live together for eternity, in God's presence in heaven – so we had better learn to live together in harmony here and now!

---

4   Acts 15:36-41

5   Romans 12:16

CHAPTER NINE

Security

"For evil to triumph, it is only necessary for good men to do nothing" [1]

Kampala continued to be a dangerous place to be but it was our lifeline to the outside world, and it was essential for a vehicle to travel the 400 kilometres to the capital at least once a month for business, to meet people and to collect all that was needed to run the hospital. Those trips were sometimes adventures in themselves.

Once, when Dr Paul Saunderson had taken the hospital minibus to Kampala for supplies, he was hijacked at gunpoint by soldiers who forced him to get into their Land Rover, which was then driven in convoy with the hospital van. On the way, one of the soldiers sitting in the hospital vehicle accidentally released the catch on his rocket propelled grenade which exploded, shattering the minibus, peeling off the roof and killing all the people inside. Paul was quickly pushed out of the vehicle in which he was travelling, which then drove off at speed. He was left dazed but unhurt by the side of the road, but had the presence of mind to retrieve his brief case from the hospital van before making his way to safety.

On another trip to Kampala a crowd of people had gathered in the street. A man was trying to sell some

---

1   E Burke (1729-1797)

special black stones, which he claimed could cure a person from snakebite if it was quickly applied to the affected area. Wanting to demonstrate the effectiveness of the stone, he offered money to anyone who would volunteer to get bitten by his poisonous snake. Eventually one person agreed and stepped forward to handle the snake, which duly bit him. Not surprisingly the stone did not work and the victim soon died, whereupon the crowd turned on the man and killed him there and then. It was an unsettled and often violent time for Uganda, especially in the capital. It was not unusual to see an abandoned dead body in the street, and the nights were invariably punctuated by the sounds of gunfire across the city.

On one occasion Paul Saunderson and Rob were attending a conference in Kampala, at Rubaga Hospital, where they were resident in the hospital's conference centre. One evening, with other people also attending the conference, they became aware of someone moaning in pain outside the compound. Going out of the compound they found a man who had been shot – apparently having been hijacked for his car. The thief had put a gun in the man's mouth and discharged it blowing out his forehead and the front of his brain. With help he was taken to Rubaga Hospital, where he was treated for some days before he died.

However, not everything looked bleak and there were chinks of light in the darkness. On one trip to Kampala, Rob was carrying a great deal of money and the identity papers for several members of staff, in his briefcase. Coming out of a shop where he had stopped very briefly to buy a treat for the children back at Kagando, he got into the car and drove off. A short while later he became aware of a car following him at great speed and getting closer. Fearing the worst, he drove faster along the potholed road. The other car kept up the pace so eventually Rob stopped to find out what trouble he was in. A man got out of the car, holding up the precious briefcase, which Rob had inadvertently left on the ground as he unlocked the car door!

Kagando at that time had no fence around the hospital or staff houses; the night watchmen were armed with only a stick and a spear and were often found snoring loudly during their watch!

In spite of this there was something about Kagando that kept it safe. Because of Uganda's fuel shortage and escalating costs, Africa Inland Mission and TEAR Fund arranged for a lorry load of petrol, diesel and kerosene to be brought from Kenya to Kagando in the form of 200 litre drums. Kerosene was needed to provide lighting, fuel for sterilising and autoclaving surgical instruments, and for distilling water to make intravenous fluids. Diesel ran the main hospital generator and water pump, the hospital tractor and a Land Rover. Petrol was needed to run the other two vehicles, and the small portable generator that provided lights for surgical operations when the 12-volt car battery ran out of charge. So, one hundred and forty two hundred litre drums of fuel were delivered to Kagando. There was no secure store in which to keep these, so they were laid out on the grass behind our home in the compound. By the time this supply was finished, fuel was once again freely available in Uganda.

An Arab trader in Kasese, Fais Mohammed, who had a successful business that had somehow survived President Idi Amin's rule, was always friendly, and helpful towards Kagando but one day he approached the hospital asking for our help. He was probably the only person in Kasese to own a television and video recorder. Terrified about the risk of armed theft, he came to Kagando and asked if he could leave his precious equipment in our home for safekeeping. As an incentive, he invited those at Kagando to watch his one and only video, which promoted the Islamic faith!

The police too, asked that they be allowed to leave their vehicles at Kagando to avoid them being hijacked. For a while, Kagando felt very rich – an excellent supply of fuel, the district's one and only video recorder with television set, and the entire fleet of police vehicles in the district which consisted of two pickups. And somehow, at a time of banditry and unrest, God kept it all safe. We had no weapons, and there was not even a fence around the compound at that time.

The new government gradually started to make changes to restore prosperity and peace. As part of this process it was announced that all currency notes with President Idi Amin's head would be withdrawn, and replaced with new notes. Over a two-day period, all the old notes were to be taken to a bank, and exchanged for new notes.

Predictably, there was panic. It was a strictly cash-only economy, and in times of war, poor people kept all that they had either on their person, or in their homes. Rural people frequently lived many miles from their local bank. Furthermore, the invading Tanzanian army had blown up Kasese's only bank in 1979 and it remained a broken, charred, empty shell. The only other bank in the area was in the copper mining town of Kilembe, 10 kilometres from Kasese, up towards the Rwenzori Mountains.

Kasese's only bank in 1980.

At Kagando, it was agreed that all the hospital's cash, and that of the staff, patients and relatives, should be gathered up and taken all together to the bank. Bonny Baluku, the hospital manager, did a wonderful job collecting all the scruffy and torn notes, which together filled four large suitcases. Lois and Rob took them all to Kilembe on the first day allocated for the exchange to new notes. The survival of the hospital as well the livelihood of hundreds of people depended on this trip.

Arriving at Kilembe, Lois and Rob encountered a problem; the only bank, a small separate building, was completely besieged by a large crowd of people, all desperate to exchange their about-to-be worthless currency for the new notes. The closest they could get to the bank was about 50 metres or more. Tension was high, anxiety and despair not far away. Lois and Rob tried to find some way of communicating with the bank, but there was no possibility of getting a messenger through that crowd. Although there was no national telephone network, they did find that there was a local private Kilembe Mines telephone network, set up by the mining company. They located a telephone connected to this network, and managed to get through to the bank. Explaining their predicament, and the vital importance of keeping the hospital running, they found a sympathetic ear, and the manager promised to do what he could to help.

A group of armed Ugandan soldiers who were guarding the bank were asked to create a channel through the crowd for Lois and Rob to get in with their precious load.

Feeling very conspicuous, they struggled through the gap created by the soldiers, with the suitcases full of old notes, and emerged some while later with their new Ugandan shillings. Not a note was lost, and no bribe requested or paid. The next day the news came through that during that very night a group of Rwenzururu soldiers had successfully stormed the bank, and stolen all the remaining new currency. Had the exchange been left to the second possible day, there would have been nothing left.

Life was busy and each day we were treating patients in the hospital, struggling to get supplies, maintaining equipment, keeping a water supply running etc and there was little time or energy left to step back and take stock. But we did stop from time to time – weekly to meet as a group of missionaries to pray together, daily in the morning prayers with the hospital staff, and again weekly with the management team to pray and plan. And whenever we paused, we remembered events like this at Kilembe, and we were overwhelmed by the experience of God's protection and provision for our needs.

There was a sense of an invisible, but omnipotent hand of a loving God who saw to it that the right people and right circumstances came together to prevent disaster, to keep Kagando functioning as a place where those in desperate need could find care and compassion. The stories of that currency exchange, and of the paraplegic Rwenzururu soldier, are known and can be told, but there were many others, mostly unseen and untold.

Security was haphazard. An armed robbery beside the hospital one night resulted in the two suspects being beaten to death near the scene of the crime. The shops were empty and the incentive to steal was enormous. TEAR Fund raised the idea that Cliff Richard might come to visit us at Kagando and another project in Kampala, but it was decided that it was not safe enough, though he did eventually come in 1993.

Uganda's economy was in ruins, and to get a meaningful price for cash crops it was necessary to take them across the border into Congo – just about 15 kilometres away from Kagando as the crow flies. There were paths over the southern foothills of the Ruwenzori Mountains so, there was a steady night time stream of men carrying sacks of dried coffee beans over the mountains. Some of those men were our hospital staff members, and we could sympathise with their sleepiness the next day. On Lake Edward, 20 kilometres south of Kagando, it was also possible to see large collections of drums of fuel being floated across to the Congo border on the other side. Conveniently, as fuel is a little lighter than water, these drums floated just under the water's surface. On careful inspection one could just see tell-tale ripples spreading a long way out behind what otherwise appeared to be an innocent looking fishing boat, moving West at a strangely slow pace! On one occasion, we went down to "Pelican Point", on the shore of Lake Edward, a favourite place that we loved to escape to sometimes at the weekends. As we approached the lakeside, we were startled to see what appeared to be a saloon car sitting at a slight angle on the water about 100 metres from the lake edge. Looking more closely we saw the bow and stern of the fishing boat, which had sunk under its contraband load in shallow waters!

Living out in a rural area we escaped many of the horrors of the brutal years of President Obote. However, rebel activity under the leadership of Yoweri Museveni gained momentum in the western part of Uganda. They were a disciplined group, never staying more than one night in any one place, eating their chickens raw so that they could be ready for action at any time, and avoiding any smoke from fires, which might reveal their positions. They once commandeered one of our hospital vehicles, but returned it a few days later, clean and full of fuel. There were times when we knew that there was a significant risk of conflict spilling over in the area around Kagando. At those times, along with other people, we had an emergency bag packed in case we had to leave in a hurry to escape into the mountains, but we were glad not to have to use it.

Finally in 1986 Museveni became president of Uganda, and life at Kagando became more secure – for a while.

CHAPTER TEN

Cholera
Clean water

*"I have often been driven to my knees in prayer,
because there was nowhere else to go."* [1]

The young man walking past the hospital was with a small group of students from a nearby secondary school. He was taller than average, strong and well built, and was the son of Joel, one of the senior staff in the hospital.

Young child brought into hospital at death's door a few hours previously, now, after Intravenous fluids, well on the way to recovery.

1   Abraham Lincoln

This lad had unhelpful friends who argued that the preventive health advice being given by the hospital (particularly the need to only drink safe, clean water, and always use latrines) was wrong and they encouraged others to adopt their same lifestyle of carefree living. They argued that the "wazungu" (white people) just wanted to dominate Africans, and that their advice to drink only clean or treated water would lead to Africans becoming weak, and not developing immunity and strength.

On this particular occasion, it was a great sadness for all the staff when, only two to three hours after being seen walking past, looking fit and strong, this young man was carried back into the hospital by his friends. He had suffered a devastating attack of cholera, and was now moribund. There were barely any signs of life, and all attempts at resuscitation and fluid replacement by intravenous fluids by means of a "cut down" onto a vein failed, and he died. This vicious disease of cholera "drove us to prayer".

In 1979 the epidemic of cholera in that region was breaking out again; hospital wards were full and overflowing with patients suffering from the disease. When all the beds and floor space were taken up, patients were treated under the eaves around buildings, or under trees, with intravenous fluid bottles suspended from gutters, makeshift stands, or whatever could be found to do the job. The cholera epidemic led to many hundreds, perhaps thousands, dying in the community. However, if patients were alive when they arrived at the hospital, their lives could usually be saved.

A team of nurse aids constantly monitored all the patients trying to give the lifesaving fluids orally or intravenously. They would go from person to person,

Patients with cholera lying on any available floor space.

checking their condition and feeling for a pulse. If the pulse could be felt, the patient was encouraged to keep drinking the oral rehydration fluid (a mixture of salt and sugar in clean water), which was made in large quantities and kept in five litre jerry cans beside each patient. The relatives were told to watch how much fluid the patients were losing in vomit and diarrhoea, and then to ensure that they drank as least as much again of the rehydration fluid. They were urged to keep drinking even if the patient vomited constantly, since small amounts of the fluid taken by mouth, would be absorbed into their system even if only kept down for very short periods at a time. (The smell of cholera vomitus and stool – both of which look much the same, described as 'rice water' in the textbooks – was strong and characteristic – I can still smell it as I write about it!).

However, when the health worker, on their frequent rounds, felt the patient's wrist, it was often not possible to feel a pulse because the person had become too dehydrated, their blood pressure had dropped, and all the blood vessels were in danger of collapsing. This was now the time to establish fluid input intravenously. In those days before AIDS and HIV, or CJD (Creutzfeldt-Jacob Disease – otherwise known as "mad cow disease"), or much knowledge of other blood borne disease, we used re-usable stainless steel intravenous needles inserted into a vein. The bottles of intravenous fluids, which again were reusable glass containers, were then connected. Often the patient was so dehydrated that it was impossible to find a vein without doing a "cut down". This involved cutting the skin with a knife at the wrist, elbow or just above the ankle, identifying a vein, and inserting the needle into it. Many of the health workers became very skilled at performing these life saving procedures. It was hugely gratifying to see patients recover incredibly quickly from this lethal, but otherwise short lived and usually self limiting disease, once they were rehydrated.

At that time the hospital was not able to buy intravenous fluids, so Kagando made its own supply of distilled water to make them up. There was no elaborate still; instead an old domestic pressure cooker was adapted, connecting it to a coil of copper pipe. Water was boiled, using kerosene to heat it, and steam passed through the copper pipe. Draped over the pipe were rags, and it was the job of an attendant to drip water onto these rags in order to cool the steam. The resulting distilled water was mixed with carefully measured salt and sugar, filtered, and then autoclaved. This was a time consuming way to get the distilled water, so when it rained, water was collected from the corrugated iron roofs. After first allowing the initial rain to wash the roofs, it was filtered and treated in the same way, to make intravenous fluids.

These procedures, like so many things at Kagando at that time, were set up by Keith Waddell, with other missionaries, showing incredible resourcefulness, and a determination to do whatever could be done to treat and save lives. Many hundreds of people lived, and still live today because of the faithful dedication of Kagando's team of workers at that time. That particular outbreak lasted for more than a year and several patients were admitted each day with cholera.

The underlying, overwhelming, need however, was for prevention – not only to prevent cholera epidemics like this, but the typhoid, dysentery and hepatitis A, which were (and to some extent still are) so very prevalent. They caused much suffering and many deaths. Cholera vaccine was available, but it had limited effectiveness. The team at Kagando made a deliberate choice not to be vaccinated because of the risk that it would give a false sense of security. Sometimes it seemed as though there was no such thing as clean water, or safe food; the idea of turning on a tap and being able to drink the water that came from it was a distant dream! The communities around us desperately needed clean water.

"Hey there! All who are thirsty, come to the water! Are you penniless? Come anyway – buy and eat! Come, buy your drinks, buy wine and milk. Buy without money – everything's free" – These words from Isaiah chapter 55 verse 1 (*The Message* version) were tantalising. Could God provide clean water to meet this need?

The technical team from African Inland Mission who visited in 1979 had an exciting idea, which was to have far reaching consequences for the future of the hospital, the local communities, and the meeting of this pressing need to prevent water borne disease.

Doc Jim Propst was seen looking long and hard at the mountain side so close to Kagando. He put the palm of his hand up, holding it horizontally against his eyebrows, trying to judge the altitude of the lower slopes of the mountain in relation to Kagando itself. He became convinced that, even though Kagando was built on the side of a hill, the altitude of those lower slopes of the mountain was higher than that of Kagando, with a dip in the land between them. Were there springs of water on that mountainside? Yes! So, what if those springs were protected, and the water from a collection of springs brought together into a holding tank and then piped to Kagando by gravity? Yes!

"Doc" went back to the workshops outside Nairobi, and planned a gravity feed water supply system that would bring safe, clean water not only to the hospital, but also to the people living all around. It was later implemented, step by step. Local people shared in the work of digging trenches for the pipes, and in return each community received a standpipe, and a free supply of the clean water. The water was tested and proven clean and safe, although limited in quantity; people were urged to keep it for drinking only, and not to waste it on other uses.

Statistics showed that there was a dramatic drop in the number of people getting water borne diseases in the areas where they could access the spring water, especially amongst the children. The number of standpoints spread further and further into new communities, thus improving the health and lifestyle of the villagers.

Many years later, a friend of Dr Roy Shaffer's[2], Dr Joe Bamford[3], became involved with this project of providing clean water for the benefit of more people. With the ongoing support of his organisation, Kagando Foundation (See www.kagando.org), this water supply is still being extended. Gravity fed, clean water is now accessible to over 250,000 people and this in turn has led to improved health. Kagando Foundation continues to generously fund the programme, which in turn continues to be developed in consultation and co-operation with the Uganda Government agencies responsible for water supply and waste disposal.

The most recent spring to be capped (in 2013/2014) will bring clean water to an area occupied by 26,000 people stretching down to Kabirizi, 15 kilometres from Kagando, when it is completed. Each community is responsible for the manual labour involved in digging the trenches, and carrying the sand and stones needed to cap the spring and build the reservoir tank. The hospital brings in the materials and expertise needed to complete the work.

The work will never be "done". The quantity and extent of clean water supplies will need continual development and improvement. The population is growing extremely rapidly as are the inappropriate

---

2   Dr Roy Shaffer grew up in Kenya, the son of missionary parents, and went to the same mission school as Rob's father, Philip Morris. He brought a wealth of experience, skill and knowledge to the development of Kagando, and served as a member of the KARUDEC Board of Governors for some years.

3   Dr Joe Bamford, retired Gynaecologist in the USA, who, with his wife Sue, has worked tirelessly to support work at Kagando. He is chair of the Kagando Foundation.

demands for more water by some individuals living in the area. The original aim of the programme was to supply drinking water only, but this is being abused by the more wealthy and privileged members of society, which leaves the poorer people without an adequate source of clean water. Sometimes there are technical difficulties, and damage to pipes incurred by farmers, builders or road workers – or just age – and these need repairing. The water is God given and free; great generosity and technical expertise has made it available but people now have to take responsibility for its sustainable and just use, for today and for future generations.

There is an urgent need for continuing and deepening co-operation with government agencies, and for communities themselves to take responsibility for maintaining and extending this vital resource. Other agencies have been involved in the provision of clean, or cleaner, water, often with good results, through use of sand filters, or wells. There has sometimes been a failure, however, to co-operate with and build on the 35 years of experience now accumulated under the "Kagando Scheme". With better co-operation, integration with what is already being done in conjunction with government agencies, and perhaps a willingness to listen, acknowledge existing leadership, and ask before acting, these newer initiatives could be both more effective, and more sustainable, while at the same time enhancing the proven benefits of the Kagando Scheme.

Being in the foothills of the mountains, the area is blessed with several rivers as well as the springs. Much work has been done to encourage people to use sand filters to purify the water from the rivers. These too have contributed in lowering the incidences of typhoid, cholera and other water borne diseases.

CHAPTER ELEVEN

Community health programme

"Trust God and do the next thing" [1]

"Without God we cannot; without us He will not" [2]

The cholera epidemic in 1979 was the springboard for leading church members of three local communities, Kisinga, Kajwenge and Kyarumba to come to Kagando to make a request. Would staff from Kagando please teach the messages of preventive health to people in the community? They were desperate to know ways to stop the epidemic of cholera.

We at Kagando saw in this request a great opportunity. Much was being written and said at the time about the fundamental importance of preventative health care. "Community Health" in the late 1970's was a buzz phrase, and Kagando, with TEAR Fund support, were fully signed up to this approach to health care. The dangers and difficulties of the Amin years had prevented community-based health care from being started up to this time.

Keith Waddell had instituted a programme of preventative health teaching for all patients who came to the hospital. People attending out patients (500 in a day, at times) were gathered in the outpatient "chapel" in

1   Oswald Chambers.

2   Augustine

groups, first come, first served. They were taught basic preventative health, a Christian gospel message from the Bible was shared, and then they were "triaged" by the nurse aids. From there they were seen by a 'writer' (senior nurse aid), or the Medical Assistant, and a few more serious cases were kept for a doctor to see. Some obviously sick people were, of course, admitted straight to hospital. In hospital the preventative health message was continued, with teaching on the wards. At the same time the chaplain and his team also carried on their work of counselling, and sharing the gospel of Jesus Christ.

In addition to all this, there was a monthly child and antenatal clinic; children and mothers came from miles around Kagando, dressed for the occasion in their best clothes, mothers carrying their babies, older children carrying their younger siblings. 2000 or more mothers and children were seen every month in these clinics. A wonderful sight to see the queue stretching way out of

Up to 2,000 mothers and children queue for the monthly child health and Antenatal clinics.

sight, with the brightly coloured, beautiful Ugandan style dresses worn by the women, no shoes in sight, and children in various states of health. At every clinic, as with outpatients, preventative health teaching was given, and the Christian gospel shared, groups of perhaps 30-40 at a time gathering for this in the "chapel", before being moved on to receive age specific immunisations (including tetanus toxoid immunisation to pregnant mothers – effective in reducing the risk of lethal tetanus in the new-born), anti malarials, and, again for pregnant Mums, antenatal care.

Thus, Kagando had a firmly established, perhaps almost unique, culture of preventative health care.

So, it was perhaps a natural step forwards, that the hospital's response to this request from the three communities, was to say that yes, of course we would come to their villages to teach them about it. Choosing market days when many people gathered in the market places, we went and taught the fundamental importance of hygiene – clean drinking water, disposal of human waste in pit latrines, hand washing, and healthy diets – an effective approach for a good diet was to encourage mothers to feed their families with foods having a variety of colours – if you mix the greens, reds, browns, whites and yellows, then the diet will almost certainly include the major essential vitamins.

The vital importance of antenatal assessment and care, prevention of malaria in children and pregnant mothers, immunisations for all children were stressed over and over again. People in their hundreds listened intently, the horror of cholera so fresh in their minds – but it was still only a small proportion of the whole community. Also, there was a busy hospital to run! We could not afford to have one of only one or two doctors at Kagando, and nurses or medical assistants, spending hours out of the hospital giving talks in the market places on market days. We were also aware that didactic teaching like this, although of benefit, was not the most effective way in which to bring about changes in behaviour... So, a change in approach was needed.

Elijah preparing the childhood immunization dermajet syringe.

Each of the three communities initially involved were invited to choose representatives, who were to be volunteers. These representatives would learn the health messages at Kagando, and take them back to be shared with their communities. The representatives were normally women, being the child bearers and carers of the community. However, the men wanted to be represented as well, saying, "Otherwise we cannot trust the messages that the women bring back"! These chosen representatives all came to Kagando once a month; there they were taught not only the health care messages, but also how to teach those messages to their neighbours and friends. Avoiding didactic teaching, the messages were conveyed in songs, stories, and role-play. Many showed themselves to be wonderful communicators using these methods. Very soon other communities started to ask if they, too, could choose and send their representatives.

Excellent advice and practical help, with training, came through Dr Roy Shaffer, another person whom God has used in the history of Kagando. Based in Nairobi, and enormously experienced, he was passionate about community-based health care, and was already supporting similar programmes around East Africa. Health workers from Kagando, John, Elijah and Eliezer, soon joined the AIM nurse, Andrea Propst, and went for training in Kenya and other parts of Uganda. They visited already established community health programmes, gaining fresh ideas and learning new methods and approaches.

So it was that Kagando's own community health programme began, and it grew rapidly. The volunteer health workers were the responsibility of each community health committee, which selected and sent the workers for training. Messages about good agriculture and animal husbandry were added to those specifically about health. The planting of trees, use of terracing and keeping of bees for honey were amongst new initiatives that were started along with "ventilated improved pit latrines" and ways to improve water quality, such as the use of sand based water filters.

To help give individual community health workers job satisfaction, and some status, they were taught how to recognise common illnesses, and when it was necessary to refer a patient to hospital. They were also given supplies of simple medicines, such as anti malarials, paracetamol, anti worm medicine and iron tablets. Each health committee bought these at cost price from the hospital, and then sold them on to those in need, taking care not to overcharge.

The next step was for the very successful Kagando mother and baby clinics to be taken out of the hospital setting into the communities, so a team from Kagando would visit each participating community on their chosen day and help run the clinic. The same pattern that had been so successfully used at Kagando was repeated in each village. Centres from near and far asked to be involved, and some health committees, such as that at Rwesande, about 70 kilometres from Kagando, built their own simple clinic buildings, using a design drawn for them by the Kagando team. One community, Kitabu, even built its own road across the hills so that that the Kagando team would be able to do their monthly visit. A regular training programme was established at Kagando, teaching new Community Health Workers, and refreshing existing workers. This programme had far reaching consequences; many of these "clinics" developed and became established health centres, some now run by Government Health workers, others remained church clinics run under the umbrella of the Anglican Diocese of South Ruwenzori. Rwesande is now a sophisticated health centre, with a dental unit as well!

All this came about initially because of the cholera epidemic, combined with a wise pre-existing preventative health approach, but also because God provided just the right people and resources, at just the right time.

One essential resource for the programme was a suitable vehicle. Land Rovers, with their ready supply of spares in Uganda at that time, seemed the most appropriate vehicle, but they were, for us at that time, prohibitively expensive, and difficult to import into the country.

However, also at that time, the Royal Commonwealth Society for the Blind (now known as "Sight Savers") decided, with the ending of President Idi Amin's rule, to bring a team back into Uganda to restart their eye work in the country. They therefore bought and imported a mix of pickups, and Land Rovers. However, within days of arrival in Kampala they had lost two of their vehicles in armed hijackings. Withdrawing their team and vehicles immediately to Nairobi, they temporarily abandoned their plans for Uganda because of the lack of security. Sensing an opportunity to acquire a nearly new diesel powered vehicle at significant discount, already registered in Uganda, we negotiated to purchase one of their Land Rovers from them.

Believing that it would be possible to simply go to Nairobi, collect the vehicle, and drive back to Kagando, Rob travelled the 700 miles to Nairobi by bus and taxi. The Land Rover seemed to be everything that Kagando prayed for – almost unused and equipped with an extra fuel tank. Buying a few supplies in Nairobi, and arranging for the obligatory red crosses to be painted on, Rob took it to the Kenya customs to obtain the necessary clearance to export it again into Uganda, where it was already registered. That was a Friday afternoon; conscious of the need to avoid leaving Kagando understaffed, the plan was to leave Nairobi early on Saturday, and get close to the Uganda border that night before crossing and perhaps getting back to Kagando on the Sunday.

At customs in Nairobi there was an unpleasant shock. The papers necessary for this Uganda registered vehicle to be kept in Kenya by the Royal Commonwealth Society for the Blind in Kenya had long since expired. As a result, Rob was told, Kenya duty (around 100% of the value of the vehicle) and a fine were to be paid before the Land Rover could be released. It was immediately impounded in the customs compound, and locked. It was Friday afternoon.

Rob made heart-felt pleas to the customs officials there but to no avail. They were sympathetic, but the rules had been breached, and they could neither release the vehicle, nor issue the papers for it to be taken back in Uganda. Rob would, he was told, have to wait until after the weekend to speak to a senior customs official to negotiate the fees to be paid in line with an agreed value for the vehicle. To him it seemed clear that the money spent (around £8,700 – a huge sum at that time) was probably wasted and the car would have to be abandoned. The customs office and compound were to be locked up for the weekend, with the vehicle and all its contents inside. However, leaving the office tired and dejected, Rob was stopped by one of the customs officials. He explained that if Rob returned the next morning (Saturday, when all the offices would normally be closed), he would see if he could help.

There was a chink of light – but was there about to be a demand for a large bribe, which Kagando were unable and unwilling to pay? Or was the official just embarrassed at what had happened (although it was no fault of his own) and was acting out of sympathy and natural gracious hospitality, wanting to make me feel better? That evening Rob telephoned friends in the UK and asked them to pray!

Arriving at the customs office the next morning at

the time agreed Rob found it all locked and deserted, as expected on a Saturday morning. About to leave in despair, the same customs official from the evening before arrived. Rob could take the Land Rover, he explained, provided he accepted that the vehicle was illegally in Kenya, and that the customs official could provide no assurance that Kenya customs at the border would not impound it again. He also warned that police on the way would have the right to confiscate and impound it. What did Rob want to do?

There was pressure to get back to Kagando, where there was so much work to be done. Rob knew stories of vehicles being impounded, and then there were all those supplies already loaded onto the vehicle. There was no obvious right course of action, but Rob took the keys, thanked the customs official profoundly. He had come in from home on his day off, and had asked for no payment of any kind. After a final check over the vehicle, Rob drove out of Nairobi and headed towards Uganda. With the day now half gone, he could not get to the border before night, but planned to stay in a town called Kisumu, with a view to an early start on the Sunday. That would allow plenty of time for the expected difficult, protracted negotiations with customs at the exit from Kenya.

The Land Rover was excellent; a Series three, Long Wheel base, two and quarter litre diesel model, it was not fast, but easily maintained and repairable, and just what Kagando, and especially the Community Health Programme, needed. That first stage of the journey seemed to be going very well; only the last few miles remained, on a long, straight road before arriving in Kisumu. All that remained was to find somewhere to stay for the night before driving on to the border the next day.

Then disaster threatened. Stopped by a policeman, Rob was accused of speeding. This seemed strange, as the Land Rover flat out was only capable of breaking the speed limit with great difficulty, and he had not been going flat out. Besides, the policeman had no means of measuring what speed the car was going. Payment of an immediate fine was demanded (illegally) and when this was not forthcoming, the policeman demanded to see the vehicle's papers, and Rob's driving licence. So he handed a sheaf of papers to the policeman, knowing that they were useless, prayed silently, and waited for the expected impounding.

Clearly, however, the policeman did not understand the papers; getting bored, with no bribe forthcoming, he handed the papers back, and waved Rob on. The next day, arriving at the border crossing early, the Kenya customs officials did not even ask for the relevant papers that would have been so damning, and it was a smooth, rapid process to get back into Uganda, and so on to Kagando.

Without doubt, it seemed, an amazing answer to prayer, and yet again evidence of God's providing, guiding hand.

As Kagando became more than just a hospital, it was necessary to look into its role within the community. A nursery school for the staff children started by Jen was growing fast, and became an established primary school, serving not just staff children, but aiming to provide excellent primary education for any child in the neighbourhood. Dr Roy Shaffer came up with the name – Kagando Rural Development Centre or KARUDEC for short. Over the years KARUDEC incorporated the hospital, community health work, primary school, a demonstration farm which also provided milk, eggs, chicken, honey, vegetables and fruit for patients and staff, a maize grinding mill, oil seed crusher, tree nursery, carpentry and mechanical workshops, microfinance scheme as well as all the related hospital community health outreach programmes. In 1985 the pattern for the future seemed established; the vision was for integrated good quality health care, aided by a network of sustainable, potentially profitable enterprises that could subsidise the provision of health care to a very poor, conflict torn community.

In 1994 Oxfam were asked by Kagando to look into the services provided, especially the income and expenditure. Their suggestion was to cut back on the community health work and concentrate on visiting just three of the centres – Kisinga, Kyondo and Munkunyu. The Oxfam report was acted upon, and this coincided with the beginning of another period of great instability and some unrest at Kagando.

CHAPTER TWELVE

Building a Team

*'God grant me the serenity to accept the things
I cannot change, the courage to change the things
I can and the wisdom to know the difference'* [1]

As the political situation in Kasese district became
more settled and peaceful in the early 1980s, there
were more immediate considerations in planning for the
future of Kagando, and a key part of this was to find the
right people to be in leadership. From the outset our
intention as expatriate missionary workers was to work
ourselves out of a job; the future for Kagando belonged
to Uganda and Ugandans, and this had to be reflected in
the leadership there at Kagando. God led us to some key
people who worked well together in those days of
extremely rapid change. They helped to steer the project
through those changes that were essential to develop
Kagando Hospital into a unit that was sustainable, and
which would later become "Kagando Rural
Development Centre", or KARUDEC – but we did not
know that at the time!

One of those three leading men was Bonny Baluku.
He had been working at the hospital for some years as a
nurse aid, and "writer", but he also had gifts of leadership
and administration. A faithful, godly and honest man, he

---

1   Reinhold Niebuhr – the "serenity prayer"

became the hospital manager in 1978 and did an excellent job for many years. Hg was part of the team that kept the hospital functioning during the "liberation war" of 1979, when there was no expatriate help at the hospital at all. His wise counsel, courage and sense of humour helped steer Kagando through many difficult times in the years ahead.

Jotham Muhindo, a local resident of Kisinga, worked with the Uganda Forestry Commission. His father, Daudi, had fought with the British in the King's African Rifles in the Second World War, and his whole family are still highly respected in the local church and community. He joined the Kagando team as Estates Manager in 1981 and used his past experience to build up the work on the hospital land as well as establishing good relationships with the local people. His skills as a Forrester were used to develop Kagando's own tree nursery, and he helped to maintain a healthy respect for Kagando's rich heritage of trees.

Isaac Kisembo's home was also not far from Kagando; he was an agriculturalist working with the Uganda Government during Idi Amin's rule, and remained in government agricultural service after Amin's downfall. One day, soldiers visited the camp where he was living and working in an area north of Kampala. They had been instructed to kill every single person in each house of the workers' compound. They sealed off the area and then proceeded to do their work. While some soldiers started killing everyone in each house at one end of the camp, another group started battering people to death from the other end. Going from house to house, both groups thought they had completed their task, but failed to realise that they had missed out one house – the one where Isaac was hiding. Thinking that their job was complete, the soldiers left the compound, and Isaac escaped. He was able to make his way back to his home area of Kinyamaseke, which is 15 kilometres from Kagando. He approached the hospital saying he was sure God had kept him alive for the purpose of serving Him. Was there a place for him to work there at Kagando, serving God, and His people? It was not hard to invite him to join the team as the person to build up the agricultural side of Kagando's outreach.

Keloi Kikoma. Kagando Hospital Matron, at the reception desk of the newly opened Maternity Unit. 1982.

These three managers oversaw the work of the hospital, the estates, and agriculture. In addition to them, there was a gracious and very competent registered nurse, Keloi Kikoma, who also had great gifts as a leader. She was a natural choice to be the first Ugandan matron of the hospital.

The three managers and Keloi met each week with Rob, the then medical superintendent and project director, to discuss, plan and pray through all the decisions that were needed to move the project forward. They met as equals together, and sought to find agreement, making collective decisions. Rob remembers being gently corrected on a number of occasions by those Ugandan colleagues, often avoiding errors as a result; on one occasion he had lost his temper with a colleague for repeatedly arriving late at staff prayers. The four Ugandan leaders firmly but gently pointed out that there were better ways in which to deal with the problem! Each meeting began with prayer, and where there were particularly difficult issues with which to grapple, they would stop and pray, asking for God's wisdom and leading. It felt a great privilege NOT to be "missionaries and other workers", but workers together, yoked in equal status in our different responsibilities. During that time, Paul's instruction to "Live in harmony with one another."[2] was reality for us, and a great blessing. The vision for KARUDEC, to be a collective enterprise of different initiatives, working "together as equals around a round table" also grew at this time, to be later clarified and taken forward by Dr Roy Shaffer.

From the time that Kagando was established in January 1965, missionaries at Kagando had worked under Africa Inland Mission, and the hospital was known as an "AIM Mission Hospital". By law under President Idi Amin's government all religious health units had to be under with the Roman Catholics, or the Anglicans, or the Moslem Council. No other religious body was allowed to exist. So, Kagando had to be registered as an Anglican, Church of Uganda Hospital. A management committee was set up, with the local Ugandan Archdeacon, Rev Canon Stephen Mukirane, as chairman. Decision making, however, remained in the hands of expatriate missionaries. A Ugandan church leader was to remark: "Kagando is a Church of Uganda hospital in name, but not in reality"...

2   Romans 12:16

One of the early decisions for our new management team of managers, matron and director, was to establish closer links with the Church of Uganda. Control of Kagando was handed over to a Board of Governors, which was chaired by the Diocesan Bishop. At first this was the Bishop of Ruwenzori diocese, who was based in Fort Portal, and it was during his leadership that a constitution was written and approved in 1980, and adapted again in 1996. Bishop Rwakaikara was a good man but it was hard for him to be very involved because of the 140 kilometres between the northern and southern ends of the diocese – he was in the north, Kagando in the far south. The difficult relationship between the Bakonzo and the Batoro (of Fort Portal) meant that at times nobody could travel between Kagando and Fort Portal. Even the Bishop himself was threatened that he would be killed if he came into the Bakonzo region. Following the retirement of Bishop Rwakaikara, Bishop Eustace Kamanyire was consecrated.

In 1984, a new diocese came into being, and South Rwenzori diocese was formed under the leadership of Bishop Zebedee Masereka. Rob had the privilege of serving on the committee that planned the institution of the new diocese, involving many more hours in meetings. He was however full of admiration for the determination of the church leaders that everything would be "done right", even when resources were hopelessly limited. President Milton Obote was the guest of honour at the inauguration of the new diocese. He had all of the thousands present spellbound with his brilliant command of oratory. As we watched and listened we wondered about how much could have been achieved had this gifted leader been a man of God. With Kasese as its base, communication and decision-making in relation to the diocese became much easier and more effective. Bishop Zebedee retired from his post in 2003 and was replaced by Bishop Jackson Nzerebende.

Now an integral part of the Church of Uganda, Kagando Rural Development Centre (KARUDEC) sought to demonstrate God's love using health care, agriculture, education and building. It was recognised that the hospital on its own could never be self-sufficient in its role of providing health care to a poor community. Options facing Kagando included being taken over by the government, relying heavily on long-term external support, or only serving the rich by becoming a private institution. As touched on earlier, another possibility seemed to be to link the hospital with some income generating projects, which could share its resources of administration, transport, accommodation, water, electricity, and expertise, and seek to subsidise health care.

The hospital would inevitably have to draw financially from the profit making arms of "KARUDEC" in its aim to serve the church and the community. Constituent parts would include the community health programme, agriculture extension, the estate, school, carpentry workshop, mechanical workshop, hydroelectric scheme, water supply and perhaps other potentially profitable schemes in the future.

CHAPTER THIRTEEN

Building a Hospital

*"Do not go where the path may lead, go instead
where there is no path, and leave a trail"* [1]

In the meantime, Kagando was a busy hospital with incredibly committed staff working from windowless asbestos huts which served as wards, two mud brick buildings that were the maternity unit/intensive care ward and a mud brick operating theatre. It became very clear in the early days of Uganda's initially slow and painful reconstruction that if Kagando was to remain a hospital, it needed to be completely re built.

The first step was to secure sufficient land. When the original leprosy settlement had been handed over to become Kagando Hospital it had included 100 acres of land. Over the years, as the hospital was not using all of this, encroachment had taken place, so that perhaps a third or more of this hospital land was now occupied by other parties. Some of these were connected to the hospital – staff, or relatives of staff, and they readily agreed to move, with compensation. In 1979 land prices were low and it was relatively easy to find an alternative site to build a house and plant a garden.

Other occupants of the land, however, were there because their income depended on being close to the

---

1   Ralph Waldo Emerson

hospital. Some had put up small basic huts for which they charged patients and their relatives who wanted somewhere to stay while attending the hospital. Patients frequently came large distances, on foot, by taxi, or in buses, so they needed to find some accommodation – as they still do today. These entrepreneurs had to be encouraged, sometimes with modest financial incentive, to find other land nearby, and slowly they all complied.

But there was one group who proved difficult and stubborn, and they generally occupied the prime sites of the land belonging to the hospital. They were the witch doctors, in whom many people traditionally had (and many still have) great faith. As a result, the witch doctors exercised (and still exercise in many cases) great power. It was not surprising that the witch doctors were reluctant to go, since their livelihoods depended on their exploitation of patients, and patients' fear. However, with the support of the local community, and the help of local chiefs, most were persuaded to move.

There was one man who was particularly resistant to vacating his position on hospital land. His business was just about 50 yards to the west of the road running through Kagando. Meetings were held in the community, and the order given by local chiefs that he should go, and vacate this part of the land, which was to be used for building a new hospital. He refused, and after a while it seemed that no one was willing to enforce the order asking him to leave.

The hospital management knew that no donor would give funds for building on land already occupied by someone else, and there was no point in starting to have plans drawn up until the land was available. After a while it was agreed that this house, a simple mud building with thatched roof, had to be forcibly removed and so Rob took the hospital tractor and, after suitable notice, placed a chain around the house, and pulled it down.

No one actually protested. And so the way was clear to start planning for the new buildings.

At about that time, the Africa Inland Mission hospital at Kijabe, in Kenya, was being extensively re built. A Nairobi based architect had drawn up the plans, and had also successfully applied for funding to build it. The new hospital buildings at Kijabe were greatly admired, and it was agreed to seek the help of the same architect for Kagando. There were slight misgivings; Kijabe is just 50 kilometres out of Nairobi; it is a very big, very well established mission station, with a large expatriate community and school; the work of the hospital was generally a great deal more sophisticated than anything being done, or planned for at Kagando. Would the architect be able to design a building suitable for Kagando's needs?

The architect was contacted, and Rob visited his office in Nairobi – it was very grand and in a prime location. The misgivings about this architect's suitability for Kagando did not diminish. However he was confident that he could draw up plans that would be suitable, but he would need to visit the site before doing so. Dates were agreed; he would fly to Entebbe, take a flight to Kasese, where we would meet him and drive him to Kagando.

He duly arrived at Entebbe. Unfortunately there were reports of shooting in Kampala that day. These were "normal" for Uganda at that time, and were not unexpected by those living there. However, the architect was not prepared to run the risk of the flight on to Kasese, and the drive to Kagando, so he remained in the airport at Entebbe, and caught the next flight back to Nairobi.

So Kagando had to look elsewhere. In 1981 the leadership came to hear about another architect who was doing work on several church projects in Tanzania. His name was Poul Bertelsen, a Danish missionary who had worked in Nigeria for some years. He had started an organisation called "MSAADA", meaning "assistance", or "help", in Kiswahili. His reputation was for 'good design with simplicity' and the emphasis was based on 'function not ornamental excess'. He sounded just the person we needed for Kagando.

He agreed to the challenge, though his time was limited due to his busy schedule, and he felt that photographs of the area around Kagando would give him sufficient understanding of the project to start drawing up plans. He also offered to try to help by raising funds for the new buildings.

In November 1980, while in Nairobi, Rob asked Harold de Sousa, one of the AIM pilots to fly to Kilimanjaro airport, pick up Poul and then head for Kasese, via Kisumu and Entebbe so that he could continue the work on the plans. A series of delays including the refusal for landing permission, loss of the pilot's maps and a difficult customs official contributed to them being a day late. They flew over the hospital so that someone would drive to Kasese to meet them. When they finally landed on the grass strip at Kasese, after first flying low over the herd of goats to frighten them off the strip, they were met by a large group of soldiers pointing their guns at the 3 men and refusing to let them out. After a long standoff and some discussion with the commanding officer they were allowed to continue on the last stage of their journey – the final 50 kilometres by road to Kagando. Even that was fraught with delay as the vehicle broke down and had to be towed the last bit back to the hospital!

They had an intensive but very productive 24 hours before they made the return journey with grateful hearts for such a successful trip. Poul Bertelsen proved to be a Godly, humble yet talented man with a good understanding of the kind of buildings that Kagando would need.

Some months later, it became necessary to meet up with Poul again and he planned to be in Nairobi for just two to three days if Rob could get there on those same days.

A date and time were agreed. Rob would drive to Kampala, and take a Uganda Airlines flight from Entebbe to Nairobi, returning after three days. He would combine meeting Poul Bertelsen with other hospital business in Nairobi, as well as bringing back a load of hospital supplies from Kampala.

It had been a challenging time at Kagando. At the time of the planned meeting with Poul, all were tired, and needed a break. So it was decided that Rob would take the two older Morris children, Ruth and Philip, with him on this trip to Nairobi, which coincided with Philip's birthday. It was to be a treat for Ruth and Philip, and meet several other needs as well!

The flight booking was made and confirmed with payment at the Uganda Airlines office in Kasese. Rob, Ruth and Philip left Kagando at 03.00 in the morning, planning to catch the flight to Nairobi from Entebbe later that day. The trip started well; they were treated to the rare sight of leopard cubs on the road, just a few miles from Kagando. Arriving in good time, they made their way to the Uganda Airlines office in Kampala to catch their connecting bus to Entebbe. Then things started to go wrong. The flight was fully booked, and their three names were not on the list. Showing the receipt and tickets issued in Kasese was to no avail. "Nothing could be done". Rob asked to speak to a manager, but was given the same unyielding message.

It was a moment of great frustration; so much hung on this meeting with Poul – it was essential to see more progress made towards the re building of Kagando! The children had been excited about the prospect of a flight, and had looked forward so much to their visit to Nairobi. Was there any alternative? Could they get an overnight bus or taxi or should Rob drive on in the Combi through the night? Neither was really feasible; papers were needed for the car to cross the border, and public vehicles were always grossly overloaded and poorly maintained so that was not a good option with the children. Time was running out – the bus to Entebbe was about to leave. Tired and very discouraged, Rob, Ruth and Philip, all close to tears, stood on the balcony at the Uganda Airlines office, and prayed, asking God for help. Maybe it was worth one more try to speak to a more senior manager?

Going back into the office, they spoke to a manager who again showed them the passenger list which showed their names were apparently not there; Then a closer look revealed that their names had been there, but small pieces of paper had been stuck over them, and new names written on top. Rob pointed out their names, still readable through the paper slips. The manager took three more little slips of paper, stuck them over the slips that had obscured their names, and then re wrote their three names. Thrilled at this answer to their prayer, they only just had time to grab their bags and get onto the connecting bus to Entebbe. We have always wondered what happened to the three people whose names had obscured ours; were other passengers bumped off the flight instead to make way for them? How much had they paid to get their names on the flight at our expense? We'll never know!

Going to Nairobi proved to be another very worthwhile trip and the rebuilding plans took more shape.

Back then in 1981, raising funds for Kagando's new buildings was still a very big challenge. Applications for funds were made to every conceivable organisation, most drawing a blank. However, the British Ambassador in Kampala had discretionary funds, which he agreed to donate to the hospital rebuilding.

It was time for another miracle. What came next was the start of Kagando's transformation. The plans drawn up by Poul were based on modules so that the hospital and staff housing could be built section by section as finance became available. The first priorities were for a new maternity unit and operating theatre with laundry and cooking facilities.

John Salmon, an eye surgeon from the UK was visiting Kagando at that time. He was teaching doctors at Kagando to do cataract surgery, and helping us to set up eye clinics in the hospital and other centres.

One day he volunteered to go to Kasese, to see if any mail had come on the night train. Post during that time of civil war in Uganda was extremely unpredictable and fairly chaotic but on this day he found that indeed some sacks of mail had arrived. The system used was that all the sacks were tipped on to the floor and people would look through and retrieve their letters. The only other white person there that day was Rita Laker-Ojok. They got talking as they sorted the mail. Rita found a letter from her mother, in the USA, which she opened and read immediately. In it, her mother was asking Rita if she knew of a medical project to which her mother's organization, the Lutheran Women's Missionary League, could consider giving a donation. Rita explained this to John, who said immediately that Kagando was very much in need of money! So it was that the Lutheran Women's Missionary League gave $70,000, which, together with the contribution from the British embassy, funded the new maternity unit and operating theatre.

Work started on clearing the land for the new buildings. It had been decided that the "new" hospital would be constructed below the road running past the "old" hospital. In this way, the old hospital buildings could still be used with the minimum of disruption

There were several "boosts" at this time that gave encouragement to those of us seeking to see Kagando continue to grow as an effective centre of care for people in need. A large local fund raising day was planned, and Uganda's Prime Minister, Hon Utima Alimadi, agreed to come and be guest of honour. Many people gave generously for the building project, and the occasion succeeded not only in raising more funds, but also in developing and strengthening relationships with central government and local officials.

Opportunities came to build up a good relationship with Paddy Kabagambe, the manager at Hima cement factory, which lies 80 kilometres north of Kagando, one of only two cement factories in Uganda. Both factories had stopped functioning during the war and were slow to get going again. Our friendship with him meant that Kagando was one of the few organisations that were able to purchase some cement from time to time. They lent us one of their large bulldozers to clear and level the ground before foundations for the new buildings were dug, achieving, in one day, what would have taken many weeks of manual labour.

Further help came through a missionary couple, Eb and Debbie Roell, who were engaged in the building of a new Community Centre in Mbarara, 160 kilometres away. It was a big project, with good funding, and many large items of machinery were brought in to enable that project to be completed quickly. Among these was a very large mobile generator on a trailer, driven by a beautiful V12 diesel engine that worked perfectly. As the project was completed, it was agreed that the generator would be given to Kagando. It was a wonderful gift, and worked well but it was impractical, producing far more electricity than Kagando needed, and consuming huge quantities of diesel – but it was exactly what Hima Cement Factory needed which had suffered greatly due to mains electricity power failures. This generator would enable them to avoid these expensive, time-consuming interruptions. And Kagando needed cement! So a deal was done, to both party's satisfaction.

As it was still difficult to get other building supplies in Uganda, we found it was easier, and much cheaper, to buy in Nairobi and transport them across the border, so a seven-ton Bedford truck, with a large closed back was bought in Kenya. The driver of such a vehicle, under Kenyan regulations, would have to have a heavy goods vehicle-driving license.

The ten-year-old truck was cleaned and serviced and preparations were made for it to be loaded with the supplies needed for Kagando. Rob was to drive it back into Uganda but to obtain the license he needed to pass the HGV test in Nairobi. A single lesson and a test were booked.

At the lesson, the instructor gave Rob a test drive, but he seemed more concerned about how to pass the test than about Rob's skills in driving a large lorry.

His advice was – 'Take a newspaper for when you attend for the test and place six hundred shillings (about £30) inside the newspaper. When the examiner comes to collect you from the waiting room, simply hand your newspaper over to him. And there you are – you will pass the test!'

The day of the test arrived, and Rob was sitting in the waiting room, but had no newspaper. Perhaps fearful that Rob might hand over a bribe less discretely than hidden in a paper, one of the test centre administrative assistants handed him a newspaper – it was very old and out of date! This created a real dilemma for Rob -should he hide the money in the newspaper, and give it to the examiner? As it happened, he had sufficient money in his pocket, but it was designated for other purposes, and in principle it was wrong to give a bribe to pass the test... However it was very important that he pass and be able to take the lorry with its supplies back to Kagando that week!

The examiner came, and when Rob failed to produce a newspaper for him he became very angry. Going through the theory part of the test he appeared to try all means possible to humiliate Rob, demanding at times answers to questions like: "Why do you come and take jobs away from Kenyans?"

It seemed to Rob that there was no possibility now of passing the test; so he tried to answer the examiner's questions, and explain his reasons for doing the test, but his main concern now was to work out some way of getting the lorry and all its load safely back to Kagando. Perhaps someone else could drive it instead?

In God's goodness, the man's attitude gradually changed and at the end of the test he clapped Rob on the back and in a jovial voice he said 'If only everyone in Kenya would drive like you do and like I do there would be no accidents!' With our two younger children, we left for the Uganda border the next day with a heavily laden lorry but with lighter hearts.

After a twelve-hour delay at the border while the papers and lorry contents were checked we realised there was no chance of doing the next four hours driving to Kampala before evening. We had heard of some nuns in a Catholic parish nearby where we might be able to stay the night. As the heavily laden truck lumbered up the rough parish track in the growing darkness, we were met by a tiny nun coming to meet us armed with an umbrella. She thought that we were soldiers coming to loot her home and this umbrella was her only weapon. Once she realised that we had more peaceful motives, she lowered it and let us in. She and her colleagues graciously gave us some floor space for the night and we left refreshed and blessed and safe the next morning.

About six months later we had to go back to Kenya again for more building supplies. Once laden up, on the return journey towards the Uganda border on the way back to Kagando, as we made very slow progress up the western escarpment of Kenya's rift valley, we realised that with the heavy load the journey to Kagando would take at least two extra days. The rear mountings for the engine and gearbox had broken several times already, and each time Rob replaced them (he had identified this as a weakness – probably because of the Indian made rubber mountings – and had bought a good supply of spare mountings to carry as spares) the journey time for the trip increased significantly. The border crossing into Uganda took 6 hours to go through all the paperwork, which seemed like a great success, and we calculated we still just had time to do the 200 kilometres to Kampala before dark. But there was more drama to come...

On a roundabout on the outskirts of the town of Jinja, with still 80 kilometres to go to reach Kampala, the oil pressure gauge pipe suddenly broke, spewing hot oil from the engine on to Rob's lap. Although Jinja is a strategic and bustling town on the River Nile where the river flows out of Lake Victoria, there was no one around who might help us in the growing darkness. There had been a lot of shooting and unrest, and no one wanted to risk being on the road near nightfall. At that moment a drunken soldier walked by, informed us it was illegal to park on roundabouts in Uganda, and said that we must move the lorry immediately. When Rob told him that it had broken down and they were unable to remove it he became more aggressive and he began fingering his gun, undoing the safety catch, and putting a bullet into the breach of his .303 rifle. We felt very vulnerable with our three year old son, in a broken down lorry, carrying very desirable goods on a deserted part of the road, in the growing darkness, and being threatened by an armed, indisciplined and drunken soldier. Tired, dirty, uncomfortable and frightened, Rob felt a strong urge to try and kick the gun out of the soldier's hand. In retrospect, it seems clear that this was another time when God graciously intervened, and cooled the anger that Rob felt. Instead of trying anything violent and physical (which would almost certainly have ended in disaster) Rob asked the man if he knew Jesus Christ. The change in the soldier was dramatic and immediate. He stopped pointing his gun at Rob's chest, hung his head, and said in a quiet voice that yes, he did know Jesus Christ, and that he had been baptized as a boy. He went on to tell us that his name was Andrews Liversalts, and was there anything he could do to help?

Rob thanked him very much and assured him that we would be fine. As he continued on his way we were so glad that God had given Rob the inspiration to ask that question, rather than act out the aggression and fear that he felt.

By torchlight (because it was now almost completely dark with that short dusk there at the equator) Rob fixed the broken oil pressure pipe, and drove immediately to the nearest place of safety which we knew. It was the home of some Baptist missionaries living there in Jinja. They graciously and generously welcomed this tired and dirty family, and provided lots of soap and water in a bowl in their yard outside for Rob to wash off the black diesel engine oil, which covered him from the waist down. The missionaries then gave us food and a bed for the night. Hopefully, Andrews Liversalts was challenged and changed by that encounter with him. But it certainly humbled us to see God at work in such a miraculous and unexpected way.

It took over a decade to complete all the buildings that Poul Bertelsen had designed for Kagando; many more have been added since then. Perhaps the most inspired of his designs was the hospital chapel. At the centre of the hospital buildings, next to the main entrance, it is the first thing a visitor sees when they come to Kagando. Simple, using the natural slope of the ground there, designed in the shape of a cross, the building has a natural "amphitheatre" effect. It is beautiful in its simplicity, ideal in its size, with its big West facing glass window looking out onto the Rwenzori Mountains (one of the most beautiful church windows imaginable!) It is a place that honours God, while at the same time being very adaptable for many different uses. It has stood, and will stand the test of time.

In 2005, Poul Bertelsen celebrated 25 years of working with his organisation, MSAADA, which he had set up to serve churches and charities across East Africa and India. He wrote in 2008: "What has been done and accomplished through MSAADA could not have happened without it having been blessed by God. Or without the many great colleagues and co-workers, who have served with me in the organization, for longer or shorter periods, for more than a quarter of a century".[2] The partnership with MSAADA had surely turned out to be a real blessing, and set Kagando on the way to being the busy and important medical centre that it is today.

---

2 *Design & Dignity: The Birth and Development of Msaada Architects* by Poul Bertelsen (ISBN: 9781933794648)

CHAPTER FOURTEEN

Building a Dam
Hydro Electric Scheme

All things work together for good...

*"A man may make his plans, but God directs
his footsteps"* [1]

It never ceased to amaze us the way that God could take
a difficult and discouraging situation and use it in a
positive way to bring about unforeseen blessings.

One day on a journey into Kampala from Kagando
Rob was stopped at a roadblock near the city. It had a
reputation as a "difficult" roadblock, and this occasion was
no exception – it was taking a long time as each car was
stopped and searched. Rob stood waiting for everything
to be checked and rechecked when he noticed another
European suffering the same procedure coming in the
opposite direction. They got talking and it transpired he
was a Swedish engineer named Enar Eskillson and he was
on his way to Kisiizi Hospital in the South West of Uganda
to work on their hydroelectric scheme. Taking advantage
of this unexpected meeting, Rob asked if there was any
chance Enar could come the 150 kilometres north to visit
Kagando after he had finished at Kisiizi, to see whether
there might be a possibility of building an hydroelectric
scheme there. Enar asked if there were any rivers near to
Kagando, and on hearing there was one, he agreed to

---

1   Proverbs 16:9

visit, raising a finger in a way characteristic of him, and said "It shall be done". Both cars were eventually given the all clear at the roadblock, and they parted.

Enar kept his word, and some while later arrived at Kagando to explore the potential for a hydroelectric scheme to serve the needs of the hospital. Three kilometres from Kagando is Nsenyi, a Catholic parish with schools and a large church. Nsenyi is right at the point where the Rwenzori Mountains start to rise sharply. The river Rwembya is a small river, which leaves the main bulk of the mountain at Nsenyi before flowing down into the plains, and into Lake Edward. It had the advantage of being easily accessible there at Nsenyi, and coming out of the mountain at a point where rock on both sides of the river provided convenient anchor points for the building of a small dam. Enar walked up and down the river, unaffected by his 78 years, going from rock to rock; Rob at half that age had difficulty keeping up with him as he marched along, doing his calculations. After much thought, questioning of local people about variations in water flow, many pages of notes, drawings and calculations, the day came when he raised his finger again, and said, "It shall be done".

True to his word, Enar went back to his home in Uppsala, Sweden, drew up the plans and raised most of the money that would be needed for the scheme from the Swedish Free Church. The project was designed to provide in the region of 70 kilowatt of electricity – more than enough to supply the needs of Kagando at that time.

Agreement had to be reached with the Catholic Parish at Nsenyi for the use of their land to gain access to the river at the point where the dam was to be built. In return for allowing this access, Father Archangel, the priest in charge, asked that the parish would be allowed to have free electricity; this was duly agreed. The sixty-centimetre diameter penstock pipe would carry the water from the dam to a small house three hundred metres downstream where the turbine and generator would be installed. Several huge boulders lay in the path of the planned route for the penstock. They were far too large to be moved, and there were no explosives available. We had to find a way to break up the rock, and create a channel through which the penstock could be installed. In the end the answer was to light fires on each rock and let them burn until the rock was extremely hot, then one of the workmen would quickly pour cold water on it. The sudden drop in temperature caused some cracking of the rock. But it was very laborious work and took many days. Before the job could be finished in this way, Hima Cement factory[2] generously agreed to share their precious ration of explosives, and the last few rocks were quickly dynamited. With the rocks broken up, it was possible finally to install the penstock.

The electricity from the turbine was then taken by underground cable along the road to the hospital, and the people who owned the land along the route were asked to assist in digging the channel for the cable in return for some compensation.

Generation of power started in 1986, but very soon there were problems with the turbine. Flooding of the river is frequent and severe, causing large rocks, and a great deal of silt (including a baby elephant on one occasion) to

2   Hima Cement factory; one of two cement factories in Uganda at that time, Hima is about 80 Kilometres from Kagando; the other cement factory in Uganda then was in Tororo, 640 Kilometres from Kagando.

be washed down, which led to damage of the fragile turbine blades. Very early on the turbine had to be modified, and the scheme never again achieved the power output originally anticipated, nor the degree of reliability, which the hospital really needed. Subsequently, over the years, there have been many challenges to keep the dam from being silted up, the turbines running, the power being generated, and the underground cables from being sabotaged and stolen. In retrospect, it seems that the one mistake was that the frequency and severity of flooding of this river was underestimated. The resultant damage to the turbine almost from the outset prevented the scheme from fulfilling its potential. Furthermore as the hydroelectric scheme has produced less power, the hospital's need for more power has increased greatly. On the other hand, the hospital and Nsenyi Catholic Parish have been blessed with almost continual electric power, which has cost, in relative terms, a minimal amount of money.

An attempt was made to refurbish the hydroelectric scheme in 1996, but it proved inadequate, and there was little or no improvement; then it broke down completely in 2010. At about that time Ugandan Electricity Board extended its power lines to include Kagando and the local community. So, Kagando had power again, but it was, and remains, very expensive, and very unreliable. The wonderfully generous donation of a 200KW Lister diesel generator has meant that the hospital has been able to meet its needs, but the cost has been high in terms of purchasing power from the national grid, or the cost of running the standby generator.

Work began again to refurbish the hydroelectric scheme in 2011. An engineer was engaged to plan and deliver an improved, reliable power supply from the hydroelectric plant. Work began to build a larger dam just downstream from the original dam, including elaborate silt and rock trapping arrangements. Three new "turbines" were purchased from Germany, and a number of solar panels with storage batteries and an inverter to provide backup power for the operating theatre, maternity and neonatal units. Optimistic claims were made for the potential power output that might be gained from this new refurbished scheme, and the plans were endorsed by the engineering wing of Makerere University in Kampala, and by other independent civil engineers. The Uganda Government Rural Electrification Agency supported the scheme by agreeing to install a new 33KV overhead power line from Nsenyi to Kagando, and they have fulfilled their promise with power lines, which are almost completely installed and ready to use. Completion dates for the scheme have been promised, set, and then extended numerous times over the past two years. Then, suddenly, in April 2014, the consulting engineer in charge of the refurbishment scheme disappeared. Up to the time of writing he has failed to respond to calls or messages.

Suspicions grew when a 32,000 Euro control panel purchased from Germany failed to arrive, in spite of numerous promises from the engineer that it was "on its way", "in the docks at Dar es Salaam", etc. Purchased from an apparently reputable supplier in Germany, enquiries as to its whereabouts have drawn a blank. The company are only willing to communicate with the "engineer who ordered it" – who does not respond to any calls.

Shocked and confused, the Kagando leadership, and those who supported them in this venture, Friends of Kagando, Kagando Foundation (USA), and the Africa Mission Health Foundation (USA), have had to step back and review where mistakes have been made. A new independent review of the scheme was commissioned and very generously carried out by Charles Swainson, a hydroelectric engineer who has worked on many schemes in East Africa and elsewhere. The conclusion is that we have to start all over again. At the time of writing, those involved are faced with a series of decisions, which will have to be made concerning future plans for Kagando's power supply.

Where does all this leave us as we seek to learn how and where mistakes might have been made? How can similar mistakes be avoided in the future? Where was the God who had so wonderfully protected and provided at other times? Had He abandoned Kagando over this critical issue? Was this some kind of punishment for errors on our part? Where is the consistency? Why should we, Jen, Rob and their family, be protected, when others die prematurely (like Rob's father, brother, sister in law, cousin; like Christians in North Korea, Iraq and Syria, South Sudan – all faithful servants of God)?

We go back to basics; the evidence for God's hand over Kagando and its development over the years is overwhelming, as many of the stories in this book illustrate. The body of evidence for the truth of the Bible, and crucially the birth, death and resurrection of Jesus Christ two thousand years ago is overwhelming. But we also know that the world is fallen and corrupt, and we cannot expect to be immune from the world. We can seek God's forgiveness for mistakes made, and we can trust Him to be with us in times of confusion and failure. Further, we can trust that "He who searches our hearts knows the mind of the Spirit, because the Spirit intercedes for God's people in accordance with the will of God. And we know that in all things God works for the good of those who love him, who have been called according to his purpose"[3]. Again, as Paul wrote in his letter to Timothy: "…this is no cause for shame, because I know whom I have believed, and am convinced that he is able to guard what I have entrusted to him until that day"[4]. So, we look forward with the perspective of eternity to guide our thinking, and we can be confident that the God who has led so faithfully this far will not let Kagando, or His people, down.

Kagando has had its times when things have gone wrong, when it has seemed as though disaster has struck – and those times will come again. Mistakes have been made, and they will be made again. In the Bible, God has not promised immunity from problems, but He has promised to be with us as we experience them, and He has promised mercy and forgiveness when we come to Him in repentance [5,6.]

Are we wrong to voice our questions about God's role in all that has happened over this hydro scheme? Surely not; indeed we believe that God invites us to come with our questions, as is illustrated so often in the Psalms[7], in the book of Habakkuk[8] in the Old Testament, and other references. We find our answers ultimately in eternity, and in the person of Jesus Christ, nailed to the cross, dying in my place, looking down and saying "Father, forgive them…"[9]

3   Romans 8:27,28
4   2 Timothy 1:12
5   Isaiah 43:1,2
6   1 John 1:8,9
7   Psalm 42:3,4
8   Habakkuk 1:2-4
9   Luke 23:34

CHAPTER FIFTEEN

Nurses Training School

'Truly I tell you, whatever you did for one of
the least of these brothers and sisters of mine,
you did for me.' [1]

When patients are admitted to hospital at Kagando, or to similar hospitals in Uganda and around the "developing" world, they need to be accompanied by a helper who attends to all their needs, including being responsible for washing them and preparing food. These helpers are usually family members, bring their own bedding, and sleep under the patient's hospital bed at night. The hospital nurses do the nursing procedures such as dressings, observations and dispensing of medicines. From the time that Kagando became established as a hospital in 1965, when qualified nurses were a rare and unobtainable luxury, the nursing role at Kagando was carried out by Nurse Aids, supervised by a very few qualified nurses. These Nurse Aids were Primary School leavers, who were trained at Kagando following a training programme originally devised by missionaries. They were frequently committed, skilled and valuable members of the health care team. Some who showed particular aptitude were trained further to become "Writers".

---

1   Matthew 25:40

A writer did many of the jobs normally carried out by junior hospital doctors in other more "developed" countries – assessing and investigating patients, then prescribing or administering simple treatments.

The certificate of completion of training, which they received was only recognised by Kagando and a few other mission hospitals. Although the training was basic, it formed a good foundation for the many who would go on to further education. Some are now principal tutors, responsible for training nurses and laboratory students, clinical officers and instructors, matrons, registered nurses and midwives.

In the early days many of the young people in the programme had left school because their parents could not afford the school fees. These people now want to return to the education that they missed out on when they were children years before. It is not uncommon to find parent and child in the same class.

Keloi Kikoma, Kagando's matron for many years from 1980, instilled good practice, discipline and hard work by her example and her encouragement. Her ready smile and characteristic laugh made her a popular leader. As the project grew larger she missed the family atmosphere of the early days, but she continued to serve and do further training in midwifery teaching and health administration, before leaving to work in another hospital. She and her sisters, Canon Janet Muhindo, and Zeresi, live in Kinyamaseke, and are still very supportive of Kagando in every way.

Zakayo Black was one of those primary school children whom Rob interviewed in 1982 for a place on the nurse aid training scheme. Zakayo showed great aptitude, and was conscientious in his work. He followed up his nurse aid training with enrolled, and then registered nursing training, a diploma in anaesthetics, a batchelors degree in nursing science and finally, a masters degree in nursing science! He is a senior tutor at the nursing school and a member of the Uganda Nurses Council, holding a position of respect in the hospital, community and further afield.

Maureen Moore, awarded an MBE in 2000 for her lifelong missionary work with AIM, spent fifteen years at Kagando, as a nurse and midwife, a trainer and tutor, initially for the nurse aid programme. Several of the students she taught from the beginning are now in positions of leadership. These include Absalom, now head of the laboratory training school, Antoinette, principal nursing tutor, Loi, Julius and Mary who are all tutors at the school.

Many expatriate nurses have made significant contributions to the training and supervision of nurses at Kagando in the last fifty years. These include Lorine Griffin, Martha Hughell, Barbara Battye, Lois Clarke, Sheila Jones, Molly Coventry and Isabel Kempsell.

In early 1998 the Uganda Nursing Council approached Kagando about the possibility of becoming a national training school for enrolled and registered nurses and midwives. However, Kagando did not have many of the requirements needed, such as a kitchen, dormitories, showers and latrines, classrooms, a well stocked library and, most importantly, the tutors.

Sadly some of the beautiful bark cloth trees on the compound had to be felled to make way for the new buildings, and all but two of the original asbestos huts had to be demolished. There were interviews and appointments for cooks, secretaries, wardens and tutors.

In November 1998 the Kagando School of Nursing and Midwifery opened with much celebration. The motto, 'Ready to Serve' is a constant reminder that the reason the hospital and training school are there, is to serve the poor and needy.

In September of the following year the nurse aid programme, which had been an integral part of Kagando since 1965 was finally closed. A thanksgiving service was held in recognition of all that had been achieved through the programme. It was a great day of celebration with drama, singing, dancing, speeches and feasting as well as giving God the glory for the many things He had done. A few of the nurse aids from the 1970s are still faithfully serving at Kagando and are now called nursing assistants.

The School of Nursing and Midwifery has continued to grow and develop from the original intake of thirty-two students – there are now more courses, new classrooms, a skills laboratory and more accommodation with over three hundred and fifty students at any one time.

To the Kagando Nurses' and Midwives' training schools was added a Laboratory Technicians' training school in 2010. Careful attention to the training given, and the right equipment for the course, has already yielded excellent results. The first group of Laboratory Technician students passed well and included one who achieved the highest marks in the whole country. Careful monitoring of academic standards, and memoranda of understanding with existing well-established universities and schools (such as Mengo Hospital, Uganda Christian University, Mukono, Bishop Stuart University and Bishop Barham University) has ensured that qualifications are fully accredited. There are now seventy Laboratory Technician Students.

The Bakonzo people, and Kasese District, have no tertiary education facilities, and in this respect are the least well served of all of Uganda's districts and significant tribal groups. Once more, Kagando is setting out to meet this need. Ruwenzori Anglican University, Kagando, is now a reality in name, and fast developing into a reality in practice. The new university will have two wings – the medical science wing, based at Kagando, and the Humanities wing, based at the Kisinga school of Divinity in Kisinga, three kilometres from Kagando.

As Kagando begins its second fifty years in operation, Ruwenzori Anglican University will feature high on the list of priorities. Kagando's list of priorities for the next five years has been worked out in a systematic exercise facilitated by an independent external facilitator. The facilitator made extensive enquiries among staff, patients and the local community, collated his findings, and then thrashed out the priorities with a group which included the Board of Governors with senior staff representatives, and representatives from Africa Inland Mission and Friends of Kagando. This exercise, carried out painstakingly over a period of several months, has resulted in the production of a Five Year Strategic Plan for KARUDEC.

CHAPTER SIXTEEN

Handing on the Baton

"This life is not health but healing; not being but becoming; not rest but exercise.

We are not yet what we shall be, but we are growing towards it; the process is not yet finished but it is going on; This is not the end, but it is the road." [1]

AIM, TEAR Fund, CMS, German Medical Mission and others have continued to support Kagando over the years by sending personnel to help with medical work, administration, agriculture, building and engineering.

In 1986, Steve Harland, supported by TEAR Fund, became the first director who was not also the medical superintendent. The building programme and community health work made good progress under his leadership. His goal was to develop staff administrative systems and a financial basis to a point where the expatriates could withdraw and the hospital would still function well

Andrew Holt took over that challenging role from 1992. In common with the other directors, he had to tackle the problem of balancing the books – the numbers of patients attending the hospital and how much they could afford to pay, against the spiralling costs of wages

1   Martin Luther

and all the other expenses involved in the running of an hospital. Uganda stopped printing money to pay its bills, and inflation began to drop. With fewer shillings around, and more and more aid and investment coming into the country, the value of the Ugandan shilling began to rise against the 'hard' currencies. Whereas previously Kagando had enjoyed significant exchange gains on its foreign donations, now they were making exchange losses. OXFAM and TEAR Fund stepped in to fund and save from collapse the community health and agricultural work. Both programmes were scaled back on the advice of OXFAM.

The Christian witness from the hospital extended to the local prison in Nyabirongo, through providing Christmas lunch and then sharing the good news of the gospel. Many inmates responded positively, and this led on to the chapel team making a regular commitment to visit and pray for the prisoners and guards each week. Faithful staff from the chapel still continue this support on a regular basis.

In 1994 the last of the patients moved out of the dilapidated Nissan huts that had served as wards for 30 years, and into the new hospital on the lower side of the road, which splits the compound. That phase of the building had included medical wards, the chapel, a sewage system and interconnecting walkways. Next to be constructed were the administration block, guesthouse, an upgrade for the laboratory, TB/leprosy hostel, and physiotherapy unit. Kagando is the western referral centre for leprosy under the national Leprosy control programme. Most patients with leprosy live at home and attend clinics but a few who suffer from drug reactions or complications, such as ulcers, are admitted for surgery, physiotherapy and long term care. Even in 2014 one or two new cases of Leprosy are being diagnosed every month at Kagando.

Canon Jehoshophat Bwalhuma, a humble and Godly man was appointed by the Bishop as chaplain in 1995 until 2004 when he became the Kagando Rural Development Project administrator. God used this wise and gracious servant to help steer the staff and management through a difficult time in their relationships. In 1996, Bonny, Jotham and Isaac who had served for many years and seen huge changes in the life of Kagando made way for new people to lead the project forwards. This was a sad time, when again relationships between God's people suffered, and great hurt resulted. The Bible warns that "Your enemy the devil prowls around like a roaring lion looking for someone to devour..."[2] Surely one of the devil's most potent and powerful weapons is that of broken or damaged relationships between Christians. It is an enormous tribute to many of the people who were working at Kagando at that time, and suffered great hurt completely unjustly, still continue to graciously support Kagando, have expressed their forgiveness, and still walk in friendship and fellowship with the other Christian brothers who were involved. The last words of Paul's letter to the Corinthian church written 2000 years ago remain incredibly relevant today: "May the grace of the Lord Jesus Christ, and the love of God, and the fellowship of the Holy Spirit be with you all"[3].

Medical Superintendents included Paul Saunderson (who left to become Director of ALERT, the leprosy centre in Ethiopia), Helen Hughes, Andrew Lennard Jones and

2   1 Peter 5:8

3   2 Corinthians 13:14

Paul Howarth, all of whom made significant contributions to the ongoing work and witness of Kagando in Kasese district and beyond. Andrew and Sarah Hodges were the surgeon and anaesthetist for many years, and still help out at Kagando doing plastic surgery camps from their base at CORSU near Kampala.

In November 1996, the peace was shattered by an invasion into western Uganda by the 'Allied Democratic Forces', a rebel group, based in the Congo. The ADF is an Ugandan Islamist Militia group, which was formed by the merging of marginalized anti Government groups after the fall of Idi Amin. They chose this area of the country because the mountainous region provided an ideal terrain for insurgency, and its proximity to Congo made it easier to set up bases and recruit fighters, as well as being 400 kilometres from the capital.

They quickly took the border town of Bwera, killing and looting as they went. Christians were particularly targeted, and several pastors, especially up in the mountains, were killed and their churches burned down. Although there were battles raging all around, Kagando was once again miraculously preserved. Many of the patients ran away and some staff were evacuated, but a skeleton team managed to keep the hospital running. Over 700 people were killed, huge numbers horrifically injured, and over 80,000 of the local population were displaced and had to live in refugee camps for several years. Finally, in 2003, the movement was finally quashed for the time being. During this period of unrest, Hospital staff, along with local and Government officials, helped in the relief work at the camps.

The impact of the ADF invasion continued to have an enormous impact on Kagando for a long time. Patient numbers dropped right down as they were no longer able to pay the fees and staff from outside the area were afraid to come and work in such a dangerous place. Although peaceful now for over ten years, there is still the memory of these troubles, added to that of the Rwenzururu movement, with news of ADF activity in Congo occasionally being heard, and other unsettling stories of tribal based confrontations, and these all add to a slightly unsettled background to Kagando. But in spite of everything, Kagando continued to develop.

Rev Uzziah Kiryaghe took over the reins as project director in 1997. Although Kagando continued to expand during his 5 years in charge, he had many extra challenges to face. Most expatriate doctors serving at Kagando then came to the end of their contracts at a time which coincided with TEAR Fund withdrawing their financial support for the salaries of senior Ugandan staff. This brought to an abrupt end TEAR Fund's 18 years of involvement with Kagando. Funds now had to be found to pay the salaries of the Ugandan staff. New specialties, such as physiotherapy, radiography and dentistry needed more staff requiring higher salaries.

Uzziah managed to tap financial support from British, German and Dutch sources to continue the building up of a nurse training school, student hostel, staff housing, primary school classrooms and further extension of the gravity feed water supply to more communities.

But the debt continued to rise and it became more and more difficult to pay the staff their wages in full and on time, in part due to poverty of the local people following the ADF war. Patient fees cover only 50% of the hospital running costs.

The Government built hospitals in Bwera (30 kilometres away towards the Congo border) and Kilembe (in the mountains above Kasese), which gave free treatment though they were poorly staffed and had few resources. With more health facilities opening up, patient numbers continued to decrease at Kagando. Salaries for Government health workers increased substantially, meaning that Kagando had to keep abreast by raising their staff wages, but they received no extra support from central Government.

However, faithful and caring members of staff continued the work. Regular clinics were held for AIDS counselling, diabetes, TB/leprosy, ophthalmology, dental care, maternal & child health on top of the day-to-day hospital work.

Uzziah wrote in his final report in 2002 – 'Despite many difficulties over the last 5 years, this period has, by God's grace, seen tremendous growth in physical infrastructure including renovation of the sewage system, staff housing, medical store, canteen, school classrooms and the start of the nurses and midwives training school.

Francis Owori worked faithfully for some years as medical superintendent and surgeon before handing over to Frank Asiimwe who had done his internship at Kagando and was much respected by the staff. Dr Kapere and Dr Bumbi both covered as interim superintendents during periods when Frank was studying in surgery and gynaecology. Asinja Kapuru, followed on as the next medical superintendent.

A number of the doctors who have worked at Kagando over the years have done vesico vaginal fistula repair operations on women who had become incontinent from devastating injuries due to prolonged obstructed labour. These women and girls suffered terribly, sometimes for many years, and were often abandoned by their families and the community. Retired consultant obstetrician, Ralph Settatree, raised the profile of fistula work at Kagando with the support of Engender Health, a non-profit making organisation that helps women around the world with their reproductive problems.

Frank Asiimwe and later Dr Robert Olupot and David Lyth, continued with the fistula surgery with the support of teams from Australia and Kenya. They come twice a year to do a 'fistula camp' when 70 to 80 women from near and far are gathered for examination and surgery. The camps last up to 3 weeks and most patients will go home cured of their incontinence. There is great camaraderie amongst them as they share together in their common problem. Harriet, the fistula nurse, loves the work and encourages people from hundreds of miles away to come to a camp where the treatment is all free. Most women are very fearful and worried about the uncertainties that lie ahead, but Harriet reassures and supports them through the ordeal. Kagando is now the second largest fistula repair centre in Uganda.

In 1967 a Bakonzo couple, living in the small village of Kajwenge had a third son. The two older boys were called Shadrach and Meshach so it seemed natural to call the third boy Abednego. However when his sister took him to enrol him at the local primary school some years later, she gave his name as 'Benson'. That name stayed and today Canon Benson Baguma is well known and highly respected in the whole area

His earliest memory of Kagando was as a five year old when his father was suffering from heart failure and a team from the hospital, led by Keith Waddell, came to visit him and care for him. He also remembers watching some boys dismantling and stealing a pump that had just been installed in the river by the hospital, in case it might contain some valuable mercury. In the evenings as it grew dark he and his friends used to climb up the hill near the hospital and stare in wonder at the lights coming on in all the buildings after the hydro power scheme had been completed.

Benson used to enjoy going to the weekly Friday market in Kisinga village with his family. On Good Friday one year the hospital staff were enacting the story of Jesus being arrested, tried and crucified. The staff acted their parts well, so well in fact that a lady standing nearby, began to cry, saying she thought it was only a play, and that she did not think they would actually kill Jesus! Of course, the actor playing the part of Jesus was not killed that day. But the message of the grace and the love of God, in the giving of His Son to die in substitution for all who have sinned, was and is a fact of history. And that message of God's love was clearly and faithfully shared in the market place that day, making an impression on many people.

As a teenager Benson heard the preacher in his local church giving everyone the option to repent or perish. He responded with repentance, and he has been a humble follower of God ever since. Following his secondary schooling he became a maths teacher, before later training for ordination into the Anglican Church.

In 2002 Benson was appointed by the Bishop to be the Executive Director for Kagando Rural Development Centre. He had a tough start to his new role. During his week of orientation he suffered from acute abdominal pain, which turned out to be appendicitis, and so he was admitted to the hospital for surgery. It was not easy for the new director to be a patient on his first day!

Kagando has continued to expand under his leadership. All the broken tiled roofs have been replaced with iron sheets and the walkways between the main departments were covered over. This was done by volunteer Oxford university students on a work team from the UK, and has provided welcome relief from both the relentless sun and the torrential rain. Kagando has come to take that walkway for granted now, and it is easy to forget the transformation, which it brought about. That was Benson's vision, and the exercising of his gift to identify needs, find solutions to those needs, and follow them through to completion. There were many other such projects.

There was urgent need for a building to house new Xray and Ultrasound machines. Again, that great network of God's people played their part. The congregation was refurbishing St Mary's Church, a 1000-year-old Sussex church. The church council decided to give a tenth of the cost of the refurbishment of their church towards a need in a poor country – and they chose Kagando's need for an X-ray building. The Church of St Mary with St Matthew in Cheltenham also gave sacrificially to complete the X-ray unit.

This X-ray machine was one that, although in good working order, had become redundant as a result of changes in the National Health Service, and the switch to digital technology. This expensive machine was offered free to whoever would go and collect it! A friend, Clive Graham, borrowed a lorry, which he and Rob took to Walton on Thames in order to collect the machine.

A few adventures later, including a near catastrophe when the heavy crate slipped to within a fraction of falling off the lorry, the machine was safely delivered to the Medical Mission News warehouse in Essex.

Medical Mission News (MMN) is a Christian organisation channelling the generous giving of many people into the support of medical mission work in several needy countries of the world. Kagando is one of the projects, which owe a great debt to MMN for their help; on this occasion, they packed the X-ray machine into their container, and delivered it safely to Kagando some weeks later. It needed a building, because there was nowhere to install it in existing structures.

Churches, charitable trusts and individuals also gave generously to capital and maintenance developments at Kagando. A large community hall, now used for many different functions, has been added beside the Kagando sports ground, with football, badminton, volleyball and netball courts for staff recreational use after work

There has also been an extension for the operating theatre, an excellent neonatal ward and a new wing to the guesthouse. The carpentry workshop (a new replacement Carpentry Workshop is planned) has been converted into a library with books and no fewer than fourteen computers, each with internet access, giving opportunity to students and staff to access good text books and online learning resources (essential for the Nurses', Midwives' and Laboratory Technicians' training programmes, and a vital resource for the hospital). The old badminton court has given way to a nurses classrooms and accommodation block, donated by the Danish Government. A new nurses' and midwives' skills laboratory, and nursing school administration block, is in the process of being built as this is being written, although requires more funds for completion.

From the time of his appointment in 2002 to the present time Rev Canon Benson Baguma has presided over dramatic development at Kagando, which have been a tribute to his skill and energy. He now plans to take forward the next great project: Rwenzori Anglican University, Kagando. All of this while at the same time studying for a PhD in Sustainable Development.

CHAPTER SEVENTEEN

Palliative Care

'Kindness to the poor is a loan to the Lord' [1]

During 1979 and 1980, the medical staff started to become aware of an increasing number of patients being admitted to hospital, who inexplicably lost weight, wasted away over several weeks or months and then died. Many of them were previously fit young adults.

Over the coming months they started hearing about a disease that had first been seen in the Congo, not many miles West from Kagando. Usually spread through sexual contact, through the use of infected blood in transfusions, or because of contaminated needles or surgical instruments, AIDS or 'slim disease' as it was often called, spread rapidly along the East/West trade route into Uganda and the rest of Africa, then the world...

It had a devastating effect on families as parents died, leaving the grandparents or older siblings to bring up the younger children. In the towns and cities up to 35% (sometimes even a much higher percentage) of expectant mothers were found to be HIV positive.

The Uganda government were the first African administration to acknowledge that their country had a serious problem, and the Ministry of Health launched an extensive health education programme. Aided by

1   Proverbs 19:17

excellent specialist physicians like Dr Rick Goodgame[2], Uganda almost uniquely embraced the slogan "Love Faithfully", recognising the overwhelming dangers of promiscuous sexual behaviour. Without doubt this approach contributed to Uganda also being one of the first countries to record dropping levels of new cases of HIV infection.

At Kagando, until this time surgical gloves were washed and reused several times, until the rubber perished or they had holes in them. On occasions, no gloves were used if none were available, but this practice quickly changed when it was found that HIV/AIDS could be contracted through bodily fluids from infected patients entering small sores or wounds on the skin.

There was no treatment for the disease until the mid nineties when anti retroviral drugs started to become available, although they were initially prohibitively expensive for the average person. The price did drop and they are now, with government support, freely available to everyone.

In April 2006 a team of doctors and nurses were sent by the Baptist Missionary Society to help in Kagando Hospital. For most of the group it was a fortnights visit, but two of the nurses and one doctor stayed on for several months.

Christine Payne, a palliative care specialist nurse, worked in the HIV clinic as there was no palliative care at Kagando as that time. She was distressed that she could not follow up those with terminal illness and manage their

---

2   Dr. Richard Goodgame, MD, is Professor of Medicine and Programme Director of the Internal Medicine Residency, UTMB, Galveston.

pain at home. So she and Ann Goodman, a recently retired GP, spent a week at the Maraca hospice to learn how their staff looked after their patients with cancer and HIV/AIDS. They were moved by the love and care shown to the people as well as the excellent management of their pain and symptoms. Ann felt that God was urging her to start a similar service in Kagando, but she was rather reluctant to get involved because it would mean future visits to Uganda, as well as fundraising in the UK. She felt she had already honoured her promise to God, made 40 years earlier, to work in Africa!

The verse – 'For I know the plans I have for you ' says the Lord, 'plans to prosper you and not to harm you, plans to give you hope and a future,'[3] gave her the courage to take God at His word and to step out in faith.

Martha, the Co-ordinator of Mbarara hospice, was a great help and encouragement in offering to support the venture. So, on their return o Kagando, plans were made to begin caring for the terminally ill. Christine started advising on management and pain relief in some of the terminally ill patients.

After discussion with Canon Benson, Ann promised to try and raise enough money to buy a vehicle for community palliative care visiting. She felt sure that God's hand was on this project, as she stepped out of her comfort zone and overcame her fear of public speaking. Over and over again she found unexpected help and support, especially from church friends and others who raised enough money to buy a Toyota Land Cruiser.

At Kagando Taasi, one of the long standing clinical officers, did much of the preliminary work, recording lists

3   Jeremiah 29:11

of patients who would need care, so that in July 2007 palliative care visiting began. Samson, in the pharmacy, was a great support and helped to get the drugs needed for their life limited patients

Palliative care, providing holistic support for the patient and their relatives, was a new word for the hospital and community. With its emphasis on medical, physical, emotional, psychological and spiritual care, it immediately started to impact on the terminally ill. Although curative treatment is often not possible, staff were able to make patients more comfortable and show Christian love.

The Kagando palliative care team includes specialist and non-specialist nurses, chaplaincy staff, social worker, physiotherapist and pharmacist as well as the doctors and clinical officers.

Part of this care is directed towards children, most of whom have HIV/AIDS. Once a month about 30 children come to the hospital for 'Jaajaas Day', which means Grandparents in the Luganda language. There is the opportunity for a good meal, treatment where necessary, fun and games, drama and singing with Bible teaching. It is very popular for children, relatives and helpers alike and brings a little bit of fun and happiness into their otherwise tough lives.

The new department was set up using the model pioneered by Dr Anne Merriman, who first started visiting terminally ill patients in Kampala, and who persuaded the Ugandan Government to import morphine, something they were reluctant to do because of potential abuse. She is the founder of the Hospice in Kampala, where Kagando sends its staff for specialist training in palliative care. Her support for Kagando's fledgling department should not be underestimated, especially when morphine could not be obtained from the Government hospital, Mulago, but the hospice came to the rescue.

As this service has become more widely known, the number of patients have been increasing and it became important to co-ordinate services in the area. A district palliative care association was started in 2013, headed up by the District Health Officer and affiliated to the Palliative Care Association of Uganda. Also in that year Kagando began annual memorial services for the relatives of those who had died of cancer

Due to the growing awareness of the need for palliative care, Sibyaleghana Siriphas has become the first Kagando nurse to study for a degree in this subject. Kagando has the potential to become a training centre for Palliative Care in the future. Essential for the long-term sustainability of the programme, however, is that it is fully integrated into the KARUDEC management structure, and that the KARUDEC management adopt the Palliative Care Programme as one of its core functions in health care.

CHAPTER EIGHTEEN

NOTDEC
Nzirambi Orphans Talent Development Centre

'Then He took the children in His arms, placed His hands on each of them and blessed them" [1]

There was another event just after the time of Stephen's birth in 1979 that had, and still has an impact on Kagando in the community

A maternal death in childbirth is always a terrible tragedy; on this occasion there seemed to be no reason for it. The mother's labour was prolonged, but when born with the help of gentle vacuum traction, the infant boy was healthy. Immediately after birth, however, his mother collapsed and died. Perhaps it was due to a rare pulmonary embolus but the cause was never known in the absence of post mortem examinations. The bereaved husband and other relatives were shocked, and then another problem became apparent. Infant formula feeds, infant bottles and the means to sterilise them were totally inaccessible in Uganda at that time. So, would a member of this baby's extended family consider breast-feeding him alongside other children? There were mothers in the family in a position to do so, but they all refused. The reason was the strong belief that the "spirits" which

---

1   Mark 10.16

had allowed his mother to die would cause the same catastrophe to fall on another woman who breast-fed him.

Was this little baby, therefore, to be allowed to die of starvation? Fortunately, Jen, who was breastfeeding our own baby, Stephen, was able to take on this extra little one as well. We named him Daniel. So it was that Daniel grew and developed (and Jen remained well...). The nurses and midwives in the hospital helped us out and shared in his care at night. Eventually, his family, who lived across on the other side of the Rift Valley, took him home and cared for him. He came back to visit us some years later and was developing well.

Many people watched these events closely, and the effect was a deepening of trust and acceptance of Jen and Rob and their family. These "wazungu" (white people) and their strange customs, with all the association that they had (and still have) with privilege, wealth and the freedom to come and go that came with them, had taken on a baby in sad these circumstances. The Morris's were by no means the first to do something like this; Drs Andrew and Sarah Hodges would later go many steps further, and adopt a child fully into their family. But in 1979, in the middle of Uganda's time of turmoil, it was a God given opportunity to build relationship and trust. Out of the tragedy of Daniel's mother's death came some good.

Further impact from this awful death of a mother in childbirth was to be revealed later. Dorothy, a single mother, was specially impressed by what she had seen. What follows is Dorothy's own description of how she came, with the support of her sister, Milly, and many other people, to start an orphanage.

"I, Dorothy Nzirambi was born on 26th June 1950, the fifth girl in my family. I started school in 1960 but dropped out after completing five years of primary school due to a lack of school fees.

I was given children to look after when I left school from the age of 15. These were the children of my elder brothers and sisters who were having problems with their husbands and wives. In 1976 the father of my children was killed during the regime of president Idi Amin Dada that left me to look after the children single-handed.

In 1979 I worked with the doctors at Kagando hospital as a home attendant, in the business office, as a cook and later in the supplies unit. At Kagando I witnessed Jen breast-feeding an African child whose mother had died in childbirth. I kept remembering this scene when I saw children being left behind if their mother died during labour.

In August 1984 I was among the staff members dispatched by Kagando under the leadership of Dr Morris to help in the preparations of the ordination of the first bishop of Rwenzori diocese. Some of those with me told me about their concern for a new born baby whose mother had died and nobody could be found to help care for the child.

I felt this was God speaking to me and asking me to take in this baby and care for him. I tried to ignore the voice and went back to my little grass-thatched hut and said to myself that I could not manage this. But I heard God say to me that if this child died his blood would be on me just as Jesus' blood was on those who killed him. When I reached my home I found the father of the baby asking for my help because he had nowhere else to take him. I felt I could no longer run away from the responsibility.

I took the baby from him, laid him on the bed and prayed to God – 'Here is this child – help me for I have nothing to give him'. I went to the maternity where I found six women who had premature babies and I was finally able to persuade them to fill the glass with the mothers' milk. There was no candle in my house but I was able to feed the baby by the light of the moon.

The following day I told Dr Morris about the motherless baby I was caring for. However some staff members were spreading the rumour that it was my baby and I should be dismissed from my job. I was found to be telling the truth and soon the word spread that I was caring for someone else's baby and so I was asked to take on other motherless babies.

Over the next twenty years I faced many challenges as I cared for the children but I always knew that this was God's work and He encouraged me by bringing along a number of different people who supported me in the work.

A TEAR Fund team visited Kagando and liked the performance of the hospital choir of which I was a member. They invited the choir to tour in UK and I was able to get a place even though I was not on the staff. On the trip I was able to tell people about my work with the orphans.

One lady that visited my hut sympathised with the cramped conditions and promised to help me get a better house. When I received the money I worked in partnership with my sister Milly and we were able to build a house in Kisinga trading centre. Andrew and Sarah Hodges (missionaries at Kagando Hospital) were a great support to me too and sponsored me to go and visit an orphanage near Kampala where I learnt the importance of getting some land to produce our own food.

With the growing family I moved into a house in the local village of Kisinga and my sister Milly helped support me with some of the administration. In 2002, Janet and Anthony Johnston, from the UK, visited us at the new home and saw the work we were doing. As I was struggling to provide even basic care for the 24 children they offered to help by setting up a sponsorship scheme, so that the care, education and health needs for each child were paid for. After a few years we realised the house was becoming too small and unsafe from the growing number of vehicles passing by.'

In 2008 a couple from the same church as the Johnstons, John and Carlee Leftley, then became very interested in the project, and over the next few years John has used his expertise as a civil engineer to design and oversee the construction of beautiful new buildings in Kabirizi (12 kilometres from Kagando).

The orphanage now has 7 bungalows – each of which is home for about 12 children who are cared for by 2 housemothers. There is also a multipurpose chapel, a schoolroom (for the nursery school on site), staff housing, an office block and gardens all located in a secure and beautiful location. The design of the bungalows needed to include an indoor toilet, because if the children had to relieve themselves outside at night, there was the danger of bumping into elephants, which often come to feed off the produce in the garden.

There are well over 100 children being cared for, who have, for reasons of maternal death, disease (especially HIV Aids) or accident, no family of their own to care for them.

Some of these children have been with Dorothy for a long time and they have now completed their schooling and are in training, or higher education. Five girls are currently at University, one of whom has one more year to complete her law degree at Makere University

Each child is sponsored by someone in the UK or Germany, and money is sent out from the UK each month to enable Dorothy, Milly and her team to provide for the children. Money for the higher education costs is provided by a group of supporters in Canada.

There are now over 30 NOTDEC staff members, ranging from housemothers, houseboys, office staff, nursery teachers, drivers and a part time chaplain, who are all paid for out of the money given by sponsors.

New babies continue to arrive, mainly as a result of the deaths of their mothers in childbirth – but NOTDEC Uganda is officially "full". So visits are being made, and will continue to be made over the next few years, to the villages and families where the children originated. This is with the intention of trying to rehabilitate at least some of these children back into the community.

There are obviously some babies and children who have been abandoned and these individuals will either remain at NOTDEC, or hopefully be adopted by someone in the community. This process will create space for new babies and vulnerable children to be cared for until they, in their turn, are strong enough and old enough to be returned to the community.

So, in a place of poverty, with no Social Service network to support them, this orphanage is meeting a very real need. It has strong links with Kagando and the diocese of South Rwenzori.

For further information about the orphanage see the website: www.notdec.org.uk

CHAPTER NINETEEN

Primary School /Kisinga Vocational Secondary School

'Don't cling to events of the past...
watch for the new thing I am going to do' [1]

In 1981 some of the staff approached us to ask for help with nursery education and Christian teaching for their young children, while the parents were at work in the hospital. There was one primary school in the nearby village of Kisinga but no preschool facilities anywhere in the area so it seemed like a good idea.

There was a need to have some sort of hospital building on the upper part of the compound to stop people encroaching back on to hospital land so a small simple classroom was built above the staff houses. It had a wonderful view of the mountains and on a clear day one could see Lake Edward about 30 kilometres away with the Congo Mountains beyond.

A young teacher named Faith was willing to teach and care for these little children each morning. The hospital tailor made some simple uniforms and about fifteen boys and girls were enrolled. Our two younger children, Esther and Stephen loved to join them when they had finished their own lessons and we taught them some Christian songs with actions that are still sung there to this day.

1   Isaiah 43.18,19

The following year the same staff asked if we could add in a second class, which meant a tight squeeze in the tiny room. After two years they outgrew the small building and the children were moved down to the hospital site where they met in two little round, metal huts which were hot and airless and completely unsuitable for classrooms.

In 1983 the assistant District Education Officer, Baluku Uriah paid a visit and advised the planning committee to register the school. By the following year it was officially recognised as a first and second year primary school with two government paid teachers. Kabugho Peninah, a petite, enthusiastic lady with an infectious laugh became the head teacher of the school as well as having to teach one of the classes. She remained in that position for 15 years and always brought out the best in her staff and pupils. She laid good foundations for all the future developments, until the Government moved her on to another needy school nearby, where again she raised the standards.

Peninah said later 'on my way home from school one evening I fell off my bicycle and damaged my knee. I had to be off work with my leg in plaster for two months but God helped me so much. I accepted Him as my personal Saviour and I have never regretted it to this day.'

As the school expanded there was a need for a school compound, and so seven acres were allocated from the hospital land. Classrooms were then built for the nursery as well as the primary sections. Garden plots, an area for sports, girls' and boys' accommodation hostels, kitchen, staff living quarters, and finally a dining hall/assembly room followed this later.

Every year a new teacher was posted to Kagando to start another class until 1989 when the oldest group sat for the first primary school leaving exams – all sixteen passed and went on to secondary schools.

Children were taught and nurtured in the Christian faith in the safe compound beside the hospital. Teaching (except in the nursery section) is in English, which gave the children an advantage for their future studies.

Some of those who enrolled right at the beginning were Joshua, Ruth and Robina, the children of Taasi and Rachel, who have been on the staff for nearly 40 years. (Anyone who works at the hospital for 10 years becomes one of the highly respected group known as 'the historicals'.) Both girls have happy memories of their school life, being particularly grateful for a bowl of maize porridge each day though just occasionally this was upgraded to oat porridge as a treat, which made it a special day for them.

Ruth acknowledges that her excellent grasp of English now, is in part due to the teaching she received in her early days. Extra curricula subjects such as music, dance, drama and handiwork have given her skills that have stood her in good stead in getting jobs, including a post with the hospital staff. She said 'I am what I am because of my school at Kagando'. Robina added that the Christian teaching at the school helped her realise the importance of sharing the gospel message with friends and colleagues.

Peninah's grandson was also a pupil in the school and his memories include the good friends he made, learning to play a drum, not being hungry, helping people in need and understanding who God is and what He has done.

Madame Defrose, the current head teacher continues the good work. Exam results consistently show them to be one of the most successful schools in the district. They are working towards printing mock exam papers for other schools in the diocese, which will help to raise the standard of education in the area as well as being income generating.

Kisinga Vocational School

In 1985, Jotham Muhindo went to Kenya on a management course where he visited a Youth Training Centre. He saw young people learning practical skills, in a Christian environment, to help them prepare for the future by having an income generating trade.

On his return to Kagando he shared his experiences with his wife, Elizabeth, who was the president of the Mothers' Union in the parish, and she passed on the news to the other mothers. These women had been concerned for some time about the number of young people who did not have the means or the mental capacity to pass school exams and had no particular skills to be able to earn a living. They wanted to be able to help these teenagers to have Christian teaching and to learn a trade that would help them be better prepared for adulthood.

Jotham also shared their vision with DJ Devries, a Canadian missionary who was overseeing the building of the new Kagando hospital. After their return to Canada, DJ and his wife, Heather, invited Jotham to visit them to explore further the possibility of building a school in the local village of Kisinga that could help the 'dropouts' to find hope for a better future.

The project proposal included the need for practical skills for young people, help for the social outcasts to realise their potential, identify talent and, starting with kindergarten, prepare them for the future... Over twenty years of war, tribal unrest and the devastation of AIDS contributed to the huge problems for young people, who through no fault of their own, had not been able to have any formal education. Three quarters of all the children were from homes where there was no father. The programme would include training in accounts, health education, secretarial skills and workshops for tailoring, woodwork and brick making.

Plans were drawn up and money was raised and channelled through the Canadian branch of Africa Inland Mission. An area near the church was earmarked for this new school, which needed classrooms as well as space for teaching practical skills. Later on a hostel for girls was built nearby as they were felt to be vulnerable to abuse if they had to walk from their homes to school and back each day.

As there were no other secondary schools in the area, it was eventually decided that mainstream education should be added to the curriculum, so it is now a government sponsored school with 800 students reaching A level standard, but continuing the practical, vocational aspect to the school. They have close ties to Kagando and share some of the facilities to help them gain their practical experience.

CHAPTER TWENTY

Kagando Friends
TOKS and other Friends

"Now all of you are the body of Christ, and each one of you is a part of it" [1]

In 2001, a dear lady whom everyone knows as 'Toks' applied to join the Church Missionary Society so that she could use her nursing skills on the mission field. It was decided that Kagando Hospital would be the best place for her to go, and this is how she described arriving there:

"'We're on the road to nowhere" by Talking Heads, was the song that came to my mind as I made that first journey to Kagando, with another CMS missionary. As we headed west from Kampala through the towns of Masaka, Mbarara, Bushenyi the roads got more and more deserted, the homes more basic and sparsely populated along the way. We stopped to admire the spectacular view of the Rift valley, spread out before us, with the lakes George and Edward in the plains, and the Rwenzori Mountains towering beyond. We had been on the road for 8 hours before we turned onto a dirt road for the last six kilometres. I knew the journey was soon to end but could not imagine what would lie in the nothingness of that vast landscape.

---

1   1 Corinthians 12:27

It was a privilege to be a part of the Kagando community and I hope I gave back as much as I learnt. It wasn't just about doing a professional job in the hospital, but also about learning to live out my faith in the community. I demanded the best from the staff on the ward, which included arriving on time for duty each day. I did not realise I had made such an issue of this until a member of staff turned up for work completely soaked from the morning dew. She told me she had had to creep through the bushes away from the cleared footpaths so as to avoid greeting her neighbours, and therefore being late for work!

I remember a six-year-old girl called Janet, who had been admitted with tetanus. She needed drugs to sedate her, which we did not have, and she should ideally be nursed in a separate room, which again we did not have. However we did what we could and put her in a quiet part of the ward. Although the staff prayed for her, nobody was very optimistic that she would recover.

During a ward round two days later I heard lots of noise coming from Janet's 'quiet' corner and hurried over to investigate. I found some of her friends from the Kagando primary school gathered around her, laying their hands on her and praying. Janet was lying on the bed quite still, with no sign of the spasms that had been shaking her body. I was amazed to see the faith of this group of six year olds as they came each day to pray for their friend. Six weeks later Janet was discharged completely healed.

In my time we saw the end of trips into Kasese to make phone calls and hanging a phone on the washing line in the hope of getting a text message through. The mobile phone network had arrived with the building of the first mast in the area on the hill behind the hospital.

It was not long before even the poorest of people and those living high up in the mountains, had a mobile phone!' Toks Plumptre (nee Akinbadewa. CMS Mission Partner 2001-2007)

Toks was one of many who have served at Kagando, sacrificially giving their time, skills and often finances as well. We have included what she wrote in order to fill in more of the picture of Kagando over these years, and what it was like to come and serve there. Many doctors, nurses, midwives, teachers and others with skills to share have spent time working, teaching and giving at Kagando. It would be impossible to list all who have served in this way

Dr Ralph Settatree

God brought Ralph and Ceri Settatree into the story of Kagando in 2005. Ralph was a gynaecologist but he had to take early retirement because of ill health. From their first visit, through their friends, Drs Andrew and Sarah Hodges, Ralph developed a passion to help the people of Kagando.

With his sense of humour, his compassion and wide range of interests and his huge skills he made many friends. From organising an annual prize for the best student at the local vocational school, to helping with computer problems, from working on a generator to using his excellent surgical skills to treat women with Vesico-Vaginal and Recto-Vaginal fistulae, he was in great demand, and gave of himself unstintingly.

When he was not at Kagando he spent much of his time working for Friends of Kagando. He was the secretary of the trustees of the charity, and transformed the charity from having limited value and potential into an organisation that had the potential to grow and have far greater influence for good for Kagando, and those served by Kagando. He set up the charity web site, networking with anyone he could find who would support Kagando. He encouraged and helped medical students who wanted to do their electives at the hospital, efficiently communicating with them all, ensuring that they gained the benefit of their time working at Kagando, while at the same time contributing to Kagando's needs. He negotiated the donation, and organised the shipping to Kagando of two diesel generators, which run the hospital when the national grid and the hydropower are not working. He had an immense impact on the charity's effectiveness in supporting Kagando.

Ralph spent his 60th birthday at Kagando and organised a "goat roast" for all the staff to celebrate. He shared with them the news that he had a terminal disease, but that he wanted to spend what time he had left supporting the work, and helping the community. He said 'we thank God for the past, live joyfully in the present, and trust Him for the future".

Sadly Ralph died at the end of 2012 leaving a huge hole at Kagando, and in the hearts of all those lives he touched. Up to the last week of his life he was still thinking about Kagando, sending greetings to his friends and praying that God would bless the work there.

Harriet, a Ugandan nurse colleague on the fistula ward, and a dear friend wrote, "Ralph loved God and he loved Kagando so much. Even when he knew that he was not going to live long, he served us with his whole heart. Ralph was a hero to the fistula patients and during his visits he would try to cheer them up. I am surprised when I go into the community even now, that so many women that he treated still send their greetings to him. As well as being such a dedicated and caring doctor, he was also extremely funny and I miss his laughter".

Harriet was later able to make a memorable visit to England in 2011, staying for some days with Ralph and Ceri in their home. She had the opportunity to speak to some of their friends about Kagando, especially sharing about the work with the fistula women.

Mrs Rita Miller

In 2011, Astraia Foundation, a German charity, who asked if there was a project in which women could help women, approached Rita in her third year of involvement as a nurse at Kagando. After insisting that men also needed to be involved, because otherwise they would not believe the women (history repeating itself!), Rita sought the advice of Laheri, a senior nurse at Kagando. Rita had often looked up into the mountains and thought about the isolated people up there who had no access to medical help. A new outreach programme was started, and called Ruwenzori Women for Health. The programme remains separate from the KARUDEC administration, although uses KARUDEC personnel and resources, and continues to be funded by the Astraia Foundation.

Rita, with Laheri's help, selected four villages, two in the mountains and two in the lowlands to begin work. One woman was chosen from each village to come to Kagando each month for teaching on health issues and this knowledge would then be cascaded down through church and community leaders to the villagers. The women felt they were 'the forgotten people' and were enormously enthusiastic and grateful. Topics for teaching covered clean water, deworming, family planning and other topical health promotion and disease prevention matters. Each of the health workers has a mobile phone, which they use to contact the hospital for advice in emergencies such as burns or, for example, a child who swallowed paraffin. This has saved people from wrong treatment and many hours of walking.

Women have been offered screening through the taking of swabs and cervical smears, which have shown up a very worrying prevalence of sexually transmitted diseases, even among teenagers. A high proportion of those examined were found to need treatment.

Dr Keith Waddell

On October 18th 2014, there was a service of thanksgiving at Mbarara cathedral as Keith Waddell reached his 50th year of service to the people of Uganda. As part of the celebration, there was a 'free eye week' − 368 people were operated on for free during the twelve hour days of that week − over three hundred of them had their cataracts removed and could now see again. The following week forty eight children with retinoblastoma (a rare cancer of the retina), were to come in from all over Uganda for chemotherapy.

Over the years he has helped with the care and education of over two hundred disadvantaged young men, often orphaned and poor, many of them blind or disabled. When visiting him, one would often find several lads sharing his simple one roomed house.

At the celebration one blind man got up to speak. Keith had found him in Northern Uganda where his parents had been killed by the Lord's Resistance Army. He said, 'Keith has given me vision even though I have no eyesight'.

Keith's dedicated commitment to medical work in Uganda has been recognised by the Queen twice, as he received an OBE, followed some years later by a CBE.

Friends of Kagando

Very many others, Ugandan and expatriates, have played significant parts in the story of Kagando – in the hospital, on the farm, at the dam, cleaning the compound, in the chapel, workshops, administration, community, schools and those who have given financially, so that others can be there. There are many unnamed people who have given sacrificially, and have made Kagando what it is today. Above all, a debt of gratitude is owed to those who have faithfully prayed for Kagando over the years.

Jean Claude & Margaret Barrault became involved in Kagando from 1999, after Jean Claude visited the diocese with a team of volunteers from All Saints' Church, Linddfield. Taking back stories and pictures of Kagando, Margaret (a dental surgeon) caught the vision, and together they set about mobilising support for Kagando and the Diocese. Concerned at the lack of dental facilities at the hospital, they donated and shipped out a great deal of dental equipment. They have supported the setting up of a dental unit at Kagando, and the training of personnel to run the unit. The community and schools have benefitted from the teaching of dental hygiene, as well as providing a good dental service within the hospital.

Jean Claude and Margaret have worked tirelessly to support the hospital and South Rwenzori Diocese in many ways, and were instrumental in starting up 'Friends of Kagando', as a UK registered charity in 2003.

This charity continues to help towards meeting the needs of KARUDEC, and the communities served by the institution. At the time of writing, the charity ("Friends of Kagando", UK registered charity number 1100302. www.friendsofkagando.org.uk) has over three hundred and fifty people on its distribution list, many of whom give regularly and sacrificially. Every month the charity transfers a minimum of £2,000 to support KARUDEC's running costs, as well as channelling funds for capital and other costs, such as the sponsorships of a trainee specialist surgeon, and other workers. In addition to substantial funding from the Kagando Foundation in the United States (www.kagandofoundation.org) and the African Mission Health Foundation, also in the United States, this money given through Friends of Kagando has been instrumental in keeping the work at KARUDEC functioning.

CHAPTER TWENTY ONE

Effective Giving

"Anyone can be great, because anyone can serve" [1]

A s "Friends of Kagando" we are deeply conscious of the fragile nature of the economic foundation on which KARUDEC, including Kagando Hospital, is based. It serves as a District General Hospital and secondary referral unit for its catchment population of up to five hundred thousand people, including those who come from over the border in the Democratic Republic of Congo. There are Government Health facilities, including Bwera Hospital twenty miles away, but they have limited resources, and complicated cases are sent to Kagando for treatment. The Uganda Ministry of Health supports Kagando, and depends on the work there to meet the health needs of the population, but their financial contribution is extremely limited. So, Kagando Hospital is forced to charge fees for treatment given. As described earlier (see Chapters 11 and 12), part of the vision of KARUDEC was that there would be profitable parts of the institution that would support those parts that could never be self-sustaining. The treatment and care of poor children, mothers in childbirth, patients suffering from malnutrition and others in need, will never be profitable, or even break even. So, outside support is essential unless or until other models of funding, or government support, is able to take over.

---

1   Martin Luther King

What is the best way for "Friends of Kagando" – both the charity of that name and all other supporters and well wishers – to give towards the needs of KARUDEC, and above all those suffering disease and poverty in the populations served by Kagando? Should all those involved in making donations towards the work just get better organised, raise the profile of Kagando and its needs higher, increase the numbers of those who are on the mailing list and donate to the work? Should Friends of Kagando, the charity, start a sponsorship or other scheme with the aim of substantially increasing the regular funding made available for the work there?

The answer to these last two questions is "probably, yes". But is that enough, and in the long run, is it sustainable? We feel that the answers to these last two questions is "definitely, no".

Some will argue, rightly, that 80% of the world's resources are consumed by 20% of the world's population, and we in Western Europe, the United States and other wealthy countries are in that 20%. The people of the communities of Western Uganda and much lf Africa are in the 80% of the world's population who have to subsist on only 20% of the world's resources. Others will point to the statistic that shows that the 85 wealthiest people in the world own as much as the poorest 3.5 billion people. Yes, the collective wealth of the 3,500,000,000 poorest people in the world amounts to no more than the collective wealth of the 85 wealthiest. As Christians we are commanded to give. Paul wrote: "Each of you should give what you have decided in your heart to give, not reluctantly or under compulsion, for God loves a cheerful giver"[2] and Jesus said: "From

2   2 Corinthians 9:7

everyone who has been given much, much will be demanded; and from the one who has been entrusted with much, much more will be asked"[3]

So, we should give more, and give sacrificially, after all, "Greater love has no one than this: to lay down one's life for one's friends"[4], and "Let no debt remain outstanding, except the continuing debt to love one another, for whoever loves others has fulfilled the law"[5]. Jesus summed up the whole of God's law in the words "'Love the Lord your God with all your heart and with all your soul and with all your mind.' This is the first and greatest commandment. And the second is like it: 'Love your neighbour as yourself'"[6].

At present, Kagando's needs remain unmet, as Friends of Kagando have not been able to raise sufficient funds to completely cover the costs of running the hospital.

As trustees of Friends of Kagando, we have to take stock, and see how we can raise additional funds, and seek to close the gap between what is needed by KARUDEC, and what we as a charity, are able to give. At the same time, KARUDEC itself is reviewing the work being carried out, to see if there are ways to be more self-sustaining, and reduce costs.

Shocking Giving

In 1980 a missionary family were showing us around the town in another part of Uganda where they lived and

---

3 Luke 12:48

4 John 15:13

5 Romans 13:8

6 Matthew 22:37-39

worked. As we passed some children (as everywhere in Uganda we did not have to go far before seeing groups of children – Uganda has one of the highest proportions of under 15 year olds in the population of any country – 52% of the population[7]) they opened the windows of their big powerful 4X4 car and threw handfuls of sweets out onto the ground. The children scrambled and scrapped for the sweets, the bigger stronger children grabbing as many as they could, the younger, weaker children struggled to get any. It grieved us to witness a scene, which was so demeaning, undignified and humiliating for those children. Many years later, we were shocked to see something similar in the grounds of Kagando Primary School, as a well meaning expatriate visitor laughed and threw out sweets, turning the well behaved, dignified children into a disorderly rabble, scrabbling on the ground.

There is great contrasting symbolism in both of these two scenes; the well fed, wealthy visitor and the undernourished children locked into a cycle of poverty; the tragedy of the intended good in the action of giving sweets, and the reality of the humiliation and harm caused; ("Of all the foods consumed today, refined sugar is considered to be one of the most harmful"[8]); the innocent desire to "help" and the reality of the damage and dependency caused. Then there is the motivation. The throwing out of sweets in this way by a wealthy visitor to children in poverty damages the children emotionally, psychologically and physically, emphasizing

---

7 *State of Uganda Population Report,* 2012 (Reported in *New Vision* 12th November 2014)

8 *The Harmful effects of sugar on mind and body* Rense

their dependency, and creating a physical dependency to refined sugar. Had the giver understood what they were doing, they would surely have stopped immediately. And they would have been mortified if someone had questioned their motivation in acting in this way. But the truth is that the motivation for such acts is questionable; it could be argued that you throw sweets out to children in this way in order to satisfy your own need to feel that you are "doing something" (and to be able to go back and tell people back home that you have "done something").

How much of the giving by those of us who visit and give in a country like Uganda is of the destructive "shocking giving" kind, like throwing sweets out, creating and sustaining dependency and undermining existing work, structures and leadership? We have thought about this more recently, especially with the publication of several books on the subject of giving to developing countries. These books have included "When Helping Hurts" by Steve Corbett and Brian Fikkert[9]. They describe, for example, how development workers refer to the slum district of Kibera in Nairobi, Kenya, as "scorched earth", because "decades of well meaning outside organizations have made it nearly impossible to do long lasting development work there". They make the damning statement "outside organizations have poured in financial and human resources, crippling local initiative in the process".

Have we in Friends of Kagando "crippled local initiative" in the process of seeking to support and help the people served by Kagando? The tragedy is that

---

9   *When Helping Hurts* Steve Corbett and Brian Fikkert, Part 2, Chapter 4

undoubtedly at times yes, we have. Well meaning, we have seen a need in the community of or near to Kagando. We raise money to meet that need, talk to people in the community about it, and then launch an initiative to put in place something that appears to meet that need. We may set up a separate bank account for our initiative, and choose the best people that we can find in the community to do the work that we have identified as needing to be done. Almost as an afterthought, we discuss what we have seen and done with the leadership at Kagando. Kagando's leadership dutifully express gratitude to us. We go away feeling very warm inside, and that warmth is sustained as we report back to our friends and churches back at home what we have done.

A few years later we may have moved on to something or somewhere else; the funding dries up, the initiative that we have started dies, and the need becomes as great, or greater than it ever was. The Kagando leadership are left feeling used, undermined and exploited; we have used their hospitality (yes, we have paid our guest house or accommodation fees), but we have not really thought of ourselves guests, nor acted as though we were guests. We have acted as we felt: *paternal*. In their very practical book, Corbett and Fikkert give a great deal of guidance to people like us who seek to help, and one of their key pieces of guidance is "Avoid Paternalism"[10]. In a section of their book headed the "Poison of Paternalism" they describe the devastating, destructive effects of "Resource Paternalism", "Spiritual Paternalism",

---

10 "The policy or practice on the part of people in authority of restricting the freedom and responsibilities of those subordinate to or otherwise dependent on them in their supposed interest..." Oxford English Dictionary

"Knowledge Paternalism", "Labour Paternalism" and "Management Paternalism"[9]. Have we been "Paternalist"? We have to acknowledge that at times we have.

Dambisa Moyo, holding a PhD in Economics from Oxford University, and a Masters degree from Harvard University, was born and raised in Lusaka, Zambia. An accurate description of her book, "Dead Aid"[12], states: (she) "reveals why millions are actually poorer because of aid, unable to escape corruption and reduced, in the West's eyes, to a childlike state of beggary". Her book deals more with Government to Government aid, as does "White Man's Burden" by William Easterly[12] than that by small charities like Friends of Kagando, but the principles are exactly the same. In his book "Toxic Charity"[13], Robert Lupton describes, "how churches and charities hurt those they help". Like Corbett and Fikkert, he gives practical advice, listing six areas on which to focus priority when we seek to help:

1. Community – the existing structures and leadership;
2. Assets – existing community strengths and resources;
3. "Front burner issues" – those things which are already priority on the community's agenda (we have to ask and listen, not impose an agenda from outside);
4. Investing – "invest with the poor to grow local assets";
5. Leadership – support leadership development. Don't undermine existing leadership, "supporting local leadership builds capacity";
6. Pace – "don't get ahead of the people... we must resist the temptation to 'take over' a project".

11 *Dead Aid*, Dambisa Moyo

12 *The White Man's Burden*, William Easterly

13 *Toxic Charity*, Robert D Lupton

As we have thought about development at Kagando, we realize with shame that occasionally the reality of some of our actions has been no better than "throwing sweets out". We know that we are personally guilty. We also know very well that a great deal of what has been given and done for the communities around Kagando, whether or not through the charity Friends of Kagando, has been selfless, generous, sacrificial work, and giving that has blessed the recipients, honoured God, and been of great long lasting value. But, with God's help, we do need to seek to ensure that all of our giving honours God, meets real needs, and builds up, not undermines, existing structures and leadership.

Does this mean that we should give up? Of course not; instead we should, we MUST, confess where we have gone wrong, and seek forgiveness from God and from those of the communities of Kagando whom we have wronged. And then redouble our efforts to do it right.

Does this mean that all that KARUDEC's leadership do is right, and that the existing structures are perfect? Of course not; as brothers and sisters in Christ we seek to "speak the truth in love", and "build one another up" as fellow servants of Christ. We acknowledge our mutual frailty and shortcomings, seek forgiveness of one another, and learn from one another.

Conclusion

Here are a few pointers that we feel could be used as we seek to serve in situations like that at Kagando. We need to:

1. Search our motives. It is very easy to have mixed motives; perhaps only God really knows what drives us, and we need to ask Him to purify our hearts, and lead us in our motives. Jeremiah wrote: "The heart is deceitful above all things, and desperately sick; who can understand it? 'I the Lord search the heart and test the mind'..."[14]. The Psalmist prayed: "Search me, O God, and know my heart! Try me and know my thoughts!... and lead me in the way everlasting!"[15] And we need to do the same.

2. Remember our status as *guests* however much we may have given of ourselves or our resources, we remain privileged guests.

3. Respect the Leadership in place – which includes administrative and leadership structures, and church structure and hierarchy – even when we do not personally agree with it all.

4. Avoid Paternalism[10].

5. Be Generous. "God loves a cheerful giver"[16].

14 Jeremiah 17:9

15 Psalm 139:23,24

16 2 Corinthians 9:6-9

CHAPTER 22

Looking Forward

'Look not back in anger, nor forward in fear
But taking full account of the difficulties, let us
look to the future'[1]

The need for 'runners' to take an urgent message for someone from place to place has gone, and been taken over by widespread use of mobile phones and email messages. Smart 'phones provide easy access to pornography and other negative influences on the internet, as well as all the wonders of almost unlimited information. Those with access to these devices gain a new perspective on the world, and share this with their neighbours in turn. Nearly all young people support their own favourite famous football club and watch matches on television sets where they can.

Although there is still great poverty, thatched roofs have mostly been replaced with tin roofs, the prevalence of the mobile 'phone, hair attachments and the fact that many members of the local community now wear shoes – something that was rare until a few years ago – all indicate greater wealth.

In the hospital, there used to be two wards given over entirely to treating malnourished children, now there are increasing numbers of patients being diagnosed with

1   James Thurber

diabetes and raised blood pressure. There are still many who are malnourished, but only very few need admission to hospital at any one time.

In the communities, there are increasing numbers of health clinics and pharmacies. Some are well run, often by people who used to be members of staff at Kagando. Others, sadly, are run by ruthless people, who are not principled in the methods they use, to make a profit out of sick people. Lacking the skills and resources to make accurate diagnoses, they sell drugs with often dubious rationale for the condition being treated, and sometimes cause harm. But they are cheap, and people flock to them, believing that they will get the treatment that they need. Midwife led, village maternity units have been established, many doing good work in caring for pregnant mothers. All of this means fewer patients at Kagando. And the patients who do come to Kagando are now more often the very seriously ill, for whom treatment elsewhere may have been tried, and failed. Fees received by the hospital are reduced, but the average costs of treating patients, has increased greatly, adding to the strain on the hospital budget.

Alcohol has always been a problem, with the availability of "Waragi", distilled from banana juice, and a banana "beer" made in the community. In recent years, cheap sachets of alcohol in the form of highly potent vodka, whiskey and gin have become widely and easily available. They are highly addictive, and are part of a very obvious strategy on the part of large international alcohol manufacturers to exploit and entrap young people in these communities.

As touched on earlier in the book, Uganda has perhaps the second fastest population growth in the world, and this is leading to higher land prices, and insufficient land available. The tradition of parents giving land to their children as their inheritance no longer works – there is simply not enough land to go around. So young women and men need higher education and employment, and can no longer subsist on the land. The changes are far reaching, and accelerating in pace.

Instead of walking everywhere, many journeys are now made on the back of a 'boda boda' so called because of the motor bike trips through no man's land from border to border. Typical of such a border crossing is that at Mpondwe, where a distance of several hundred metres by the river marks the boundary between Uganda and the Democratic Republic of Congo. People and goods are stopped at the border posts, and allowed to go no further. This is where the original "boda boda" came into being, ferrying goods and people from border to border. Some of these are modified tricycles with hand-operated pedals. These specially adapted "boda bodas" are operated by men who have lost their legs. Many would have been injured by land mines, others through hippo bites, and others still would have been paralysed in early childhood by poliomyelitis. Pedalling from border to border, carrying as much as they can, or sometimes people, these disabled people clearly have a special "diplomatic immunity" which works for both border posts. There are strict protocols operating under the surface of what superficially seems to be a very relaxed state of affairs.

A dear friend of ours one day wanted to show us the border, and the bustling trading centre on the Congo side of the border. We were not aware of the plan, so we did not have our passports with us. Driving his wonderful twenty-year-old battered Toyota pickup, he drove up to the Uganda border post, unconcerned about us not having our passports with us. "I have my friends here", he explained. And, sure enough, the officials at the Uganda border post waved us through. As we arrived at the Congo border post, he again reassured us that he had friends there. Except that they were not quite so friendly, and he was taken away into their office, leaving us standing beside his pickup. As we stood there, we marvelled at those incredibly hard working people who had no legs, driving their modified tricycles, trading material, sandals, and all kinds of goods, from one side to the other. The temptation was great, and Rob gave way to it. Raising his camera, he took a photograph of one of those tricycles being operated in this way.

The effect was immediate; we were escorted by the Congolese officials into the police post. Were we spies? Why were we visiting? If we were not spies, then why take a photograph? The tensions rose, and our friend became quite cross with the officials, explaining that we were his friends. That did not seem to solve the problem; our camera would have to be confiscated. We did not favour that idea, and tried to find a compromise. Unwilling to pay the official a blatant bribe, we eventually agreed to pay a fee for someone to act as our guide, and show us around the Congolese trading centre. We had our tour of the bustling, brightly coloured trading centre, and were allowed to return to Uganda, with our camera, grateful for a satisfactory outcome.

But we were left contemplating the implications of all this accelerating change in a terribly vulnerable and fragile environment. The threats are obvious and great: social unrest with increasing unemployment; increased aspirations among a well informed, "enlightened" youth, outbreaks of disease like Ebola, or Marburg disease. The possible threat of invasion of Uganda again by extremist groups like the "Allied Democratic Forces" (ADF) who had previously invaded in the 1990's. There is the latent threat of tribal unrest, based on the perception that scarce land is being taken from the indigenous tribe by people coming in from outside. And then there is that population growth rate…

Where does Kagando stand in all of this?

We see Kagando as an incredibly important influence for stability, influence for care for those who are poor and in need, influence for education, and as a centre for the sustainable development of communities. This development can be supported and sustained by developing business opportunities for local people. Business for Transformation[2] provides a wonderful model for this approach, which we would love to see used at Kagando. These business opportunities can be the means for local people to fulfil their potential to use their God given gifts and resources to provide employment, raise living standards and set communities free from the vicious cycles of poverty which exist today. Above all, Kagando is and can grow as a means for the Church to demonstrate and preach of the love of God. Our God, who created women and men to be free, walking in fellowship with Himself and in fellowship with one another. Part of the practical outworking of this influence in the years ahead will be the development of Rwenzori Anglican University, Kagando.

Friends of Kagando exists to support Kagando in these roles, with God's help, with the help of so many

2 *Business for Transformation* – B4T (www.B4T.org)

who give faithfully and generously, who pray regularly, and the many who go to Kagando to serve in different ways. Elective Medical Students come to learn, but often contribute greatly to the hospital; volunteer nurses and doctors give sacrificially of their time and skills; engineers, teachers, people with many different skills, all contribute. Others serve by helping to raise the profile of Kagando in different countries, or by supporting in one way or another those who work at Kagando, whether through sponsorship of training programmes, or by direct support. Friends of Kagando work with other partner organisations also, who, like Kagando Foundation and African Mission Health Foundation, give generously for the work there.

A favourite hymn in the Kagando chapel goes:

> I do not know what lies ahead,[3]
> the way I cannot see;
> yet One stands near to be my guide,
> He'll show the way to me:
>
> I know who holds the future,
> and He'll guide me with His hand;
> with God things don't just happen,
> everything by Him is planned.
> So as I face tomorrow,
> with its problems large and small,
> I'll trust the God of miracles,
> give to Him my all.
>
> I do not know how many days
> of life are mine to spend;
> but One who knows and cares for me
> will keep me to the end:

3 Hymn *I know who holds the future.* Albert B Smith

I know who holds the future...
I do not know the course ahead,
what joys and grief's are there;
but One is near who fully knows,
I'll trust His loving care:
I know who holds the future...

Looking back over these past fifty years, we see how God
has had His hand on Kagando during some very difficult
times, and there are bound to be some more tough times
ahead, but we know that God has it all in hand. The God
of miracles, by whom everything is planned, who will
guide with His hand, care for the people of the
communities of Kagando, and lead into the future. The
God who has demonstrated His commitment to mankind
for all time, by giving Himself on a cross at a point in
history 2000 years ago, and who will one day come again.

Here is love vast as the ocean,[4]
Loving kindness as the flood,
When the Prince of life, our ransom
Shed for us His precious blood.
Who His love will not remember?
Who can cease to sing His praise?
He can never be forgotten
Throughout heaven's eternal days.
On the Mount of Crucifixion
Fountains open deep and wide;
Through the floodgates of God's mercy
Flowed a vast and gracious tide.
Grace and love, like mighty rivers,
Poured incessant from above,
And heaven's peace and perfect justice
Kissed a guilty world in love.

4 Hymn – Love song of the Welsh Revival - *Here is love, vast
   as the ocean.* William Rees (1802-1883)

Thank you so much for joining with us this far in this wonderful part of God's story, this part of His plan to bring an end to injustice and suffering, which will one day end, as "He will wipe every tear from their eyes. There will be no more death or mourning or crying or pain, for the old order of things has passed away."[5] May that day come soon!

We are enormously grateful for the opportunity that we have had, and continue to have, in sharing in small ways with what God is doing at Kagando. We have learned, in the words of Paul to Timothy, that "(we) know whom (we) have believed, and (are) convinced that he is able to guard what (we) have entrusted to Him until that day".[6]

Our prayer for you is that the story of Kagando will encourage you to know that God is involved in His world, is faithful to His people, and longs for us to respond to His initiatives of creation and restoration in love and obedience to Him. There is nothing in all the world greater than the privilege of sharing in those initiatives.

Kagando, and the people served by Kagando, desperately need your help. Please pray, give and go as God calls and enables you to do. If you would like to receive regular reports and prayer needs for Kagando, or would like more information, please contact:

Friends of Kagando www.friendsofkagando.org.uk, email admin@friendsofkagando.org.uk, or:

Rob and Jen Morris, Greenbanks, Horsham Road, Handcross, West Sussex RH17 6DH

+44 7712 658437

robjenmor@aol.com

---

5   Revelation 21:4

6   2 Timothy 1:12b

Please pray for KARUDEC, the leadership, and the church with her bishop and leadership in South Rwenzori, Uganda.

Please give generously.